HOW TO WIN AS A PART-TIME STUDENT

HOW TO WIN AS A PART-TIME STUDENT

TOM BOURNER & PHIL RACE

SECOND EDITION

KOGAN
PAGE

First published in 1990
This second edition published in 1995

Kogan Page Limited
120 Pentonville Road
London N1 9JN

British Library Cataloguing in Publication Data

A CIP record for this book is available from the British Library.

ISBN 0 7494 1672 6

Typeset by DP Photosetting, Aylesbury, Bucks
Printed and bound in Great Britain by
Biddles Ltd., Guildford and King's Lynn

Contents

Preface To The Second Edition   9

How To Get The Best Out Of This Book   11

1   Why Are You Doing It?   17

2   What Are The Difficulties?   22
     Potential pitfalls   22
     Finding the time   23
     Checklist   26

3   What Are Your Resources?   27
     Potential resources   27
     College resources   28
     Home resources   31
     Work resources   32
     Personal resources   33
     Developing your resources   40
     An action plan   42
     Checklist   44

4   How's Your Competence?   45
     What's competence?   45
     The opposite of competence?   46
     People and their competences   46
     Conscious and unconscious competence and uncompetence   47
     How will your competence be measured?   53
     SWOT analysis   53
     Sharing with other people   56

5   When Will You Find The Time?   57
     But I've still not got enough time!   58
     How long does it take to do something *useful?*   59
     Concentrating and studying   60
     Keeping to schedule   61
     Towards being a *full-time* part-time student!   62

	Capitalise on spurts!	62
	Quality, not quantity	63
	Review	63
6	**Where Will You Study?**	**64**
	Where's best for *you?*	64
	So where is the best place?	65
	Working in odd places	66
	The place to study is where you are!	67
	Review	69
7	**How Can You Make Studying Really Efficient?**	**70**
	Towards efficient studying	71
	Summary	80
8	**How Can Active Learning Guarantee Successful Study?**	**81**
	The problems of passive learning	82
	Exams test the results of *active* learning	82
	Active learning methods	83
	Getting your learning toolkit together	87
	Active learning with friends	87
	Picking the right tool for the job	89
	Summary	89
9	**How Can You Get The Best From Your Tutors?**	**91**
	What's in a name?	91
	How do you feel about your tutors?	92
	Getting your questions answered	93
	Asking questions in class	94
	Asking about assessment	95
	How does the assessor's mind work?	96
	Giving your tutors extra work!	97
	Setting your tutors exam questions	97
	Attitudes and beliefs about tutors	98
	How to improve your tuition	100
	Review	103
10	**How Can You Find Out How Well You're Doing?**	**105**
	Getting to know the right things	105
	Why ask yourself questions?	105

Collecting questions 107
'Prompts' 109
Making the most of tutor feedback 110
Making the most of other people 111
Avoiding the slide! 115

11 How Will You Cope With Revision And Exams? **116**
Section 1: Mainstream revision 117
Section 2: Just before your exam 126
Section 3: Playing the exam game 128
Review 136

12 Staying The Course **138**
Attitudes 139
And finally . . . 146

Feedback to Tom And Phil 148

Responses To SAQs, Introduction 150
Responses To SAQs, Chapter 1 152
Responses To SAQs, Chapter 2 159
Responses To SAQs, Chapter 3 163
Responses To SAQs, Chapter 4 172
Responses To SAQs, Chapter 5 175
Responses To SAQs, Chapter 6 181
Responses To SAQs, Chapter 7 183
Responses To SAQs, Chapter 8 189
Responses To SAQs, Chapter 9 191
Responses To SAQs, Chapter 10 200
Responses To SAQs, Chapter 11 205

References And Further Reading **211**

Index **212**

Preface To The Second Edition

We would like to thank the many readers of the first edition who sent 'Feedback to Tom and Phil' to us through our publisher. This feedback encouraged us greatly, and gave us further ideas, which we've incorporated into this new edition.

Since our first edition, several things have happened. First, the proportion of part-time students in universities and colleges in the UK has increased quite dramatically. Second, with larger classes in colleges, *all* students have been put in a position where they must take more responsibility for their own learning than ever before, and we hope that this book will help them do so. Third, it is becoming increasingly recognised that the most important skills that students acquire while at college or university are their skills at learning. The book addresses these throughout.

From the numerous instances of feedback we received from users of our first edition, it seems that the book proved helpful. Adopting the well-tried adage that 'if it ain't broke, don't fix it!' we have left the substantial content of the book well alone in this second edition. However, we believe that we have learned more about how people really learn – and the importance of learners being aware of the ways in which they learn – so we have added into the introduction to this book a discussion of this, which also serves to demonstrate how the interactive nature of the book is intended to help learners.

Our belief has been confirmed that the most important thing that any student in further or higher education learns is how to learn successfully – coupled with how to demonstrate that learning in whatever forms of assessment are to be encountered – particularly in traditional examinations. We hope that this book will not only help readers take charge of the ways that they learn, but also will help them prepare for successful demonstration that they have learned effectively.

We've added at the end of the book a short list of Further Reading, including some references both to ideas about how learning actually happens, and to practical ways of going about your mission of making sure that your own learning is as productive and enjoyable as possible.

The purpose of our book remains the same. It is to help part-time students (and anyone else who reads it) to discover a little more about themselves. We hope that this will enable them to study more successfully than they might otherwise have done. We believe that for all of our lives, we are learners, and that the more we are enabled to take charge of our own personal learning, the more satisfying our experiences of living will be.

Phil Race
Tom Bourner
March 1995

How To Get The Best Out Of This Book

Congratulations! You're about to become a part-time student – or you are one already. Or maybe you're actually a full-time student? In any of these cases, you should find many of the things we're trying to help you with in this book every bit as useful as if you were studying part-time or about to start your studies. In short, we've written this guide to help you get as much as you can from your course, and to help you maximise your probability of success with your studies.

What's this book for?

We want you to succeed in your studies. More than that: we want you to enjoy your studies. Learning can be fun. It *should* be enjoyable. You are likely to get more enjoyment out of your learning if it's:

- effective – you succeed in learning what you need to for assessment;
- efficient – you avoid wasting time hitting brick walls!
- economic – you've got a busy life, and can't afford to waste time.

Your learning needs to be effective so that what you learn doesn't just evaporate again. It needs to be efficient – as a part-time student your time is precious; you need to use it as productively as you can. Your learning also needs to be 'economic' – this is to do with getting the maximum rewards or payoffs from the energy you put into your studies.

We've mentioned enjoyable, effective, efficient and economic. There's another E-word: effort! There's no way round that one. If you follow the suggestions we give in this book, you should find that your efforts are well focused and sustained enough to guarantee your success.

What sort of book is this?

Well, it's not just a book at all. It's not something just to sit and read. It's full of things for you to do as you work through it. Learning has to be active if it's to be effective, so we've written a book for you to *do*, not one to just read.

Throughout the book you'll find things called SAQs – self-analysis questions. These are questions or activities that give you something definite to do for a few minutes. Some of them involve picking options from several alternatives. Others ask you to jot down your own thoughts in answer to questions we've asked. There's space in the book for you to write down such things. We *want* you to write all over this book (as long as it's not a library copy!). Stopping and *doing* the SAQs takes a bit of time, but that's the way to get most value from this book – and also it's the way to help you find out even more about how you learn best.

So how do people learn best?

Let's kick straight off with an SAQ just to get you into the swing of things.

SAQ A

Think of something that you're good at – something you know you do well. This can be anything at all in your life – sport, cooking, ballet-dancing, anything. Jot down what it is below.

Now, how did you *become* good at whatever it was? How did you learn it? Jot down a few key words about the ways you became good at it.

(Now that you've jotted down your own thoughts, please turn to page 150 where we've provided our own discussion of the matters arising from this SAQ.)

What does this tell us about effective learning?

So effective learning has to be active. You'll have seen from our response to SAQ A on page 150 that effective learning involves practice, trial and error, and learning by getting one's hands dirty! That's why this book is full of SAQs. We want you to *do* things as you work through it, and not just to read about what we think. The most important parts of this book are the blank spaces upon which we encourage you to jot things down! But what happens next? Let's have another SAQ!

SAQ B

Now, think of something that you *feel* good about yourself. Think of something about you that you're proud of. Think of something that gives you a bit of a glow. Again, it can be anything at all in your life. Jot it down here.

Next – and this is the hard bit of this question – try to work out *how you know* you can feel good about whatever it is. How can you tell? What's your evidence? Jot down a few words or phrases below.

(Now please look at our response on page 150.)

But what can go wrong with learning?

We've seen that effective learning involves practising, learning-by-doing, learning from trial and error. We've also seen how important it is to find out *how* we're doing.

We need feedback from other people. We also need to see the results of our learning. Obviously, two of the things that can go wrong are wrapped up in what we've said already – if we don't get enough practice and feedback, our learning is not likely to be really successful. Let's go into what can go wrong in a little more depth next. You've guessed it – we're going to give you another SAQ!

SAQ C

Let's look at things at their worst just for a minute. Think of something that you're *not* good at! For example, something that just has never worked out for you. Jot down what it is below.

Now, as honestly as you can, think of what went wrong. Whose fault was it? Jot down a few ideas below, then compare your diagnosis with the comments in our response to SAQ C.

So what have we found out about how learning happens?

Altogether, from the things we've looked at in SAQs A to C, there are four key factors in successful learning.

- *wanting* to learn
- *practice, learning-by-doing* (including making mistakes!)
- *feedback* – finding out how we're doing
- *digesting* – making sense of what we've learned.

We've written this book with all of these in mind. The fact that you're reading this book is evidence that you *want* to learn. In fact, part-time students in our experience have a very powerful want to learn – often a lot more intense than full-time students! So we're assuming that there's no problem in your 'wanting' department. We've written this book to help you learn-by-doing. That's why we've filled the book with lots of SAQs for you to have a go at.

We've done our best to give you feedback. As you'll have seen, our responses to the SAQs are quite detailed, and make up more than a third of the book. We hope too that the whole book will help you with your 'digesting'. Let's say a little more about this right now. In the everyday sense of the word, digesting is about extracting what's good for us from our food. It's also about the physiological processes of sorting out what we need and what we don't. After we've digested something, sooner or later we discard what we don't need! Learning is very much like this too. When we have a new learning experience, we need to sort out from it what is important enough for us to carry on with us, and which bits of it were only a means to an end, and can safely be let go of. After all, there's no point clogging up our brains with all sorts of information that we don't need to retain.

How to make the most of this book

You've already seen how this book works. We give you things to do in SAQs, then we give you feedback in our responses to each of these. How much you get out of our book is very much up to you. We suggest that every time you come to an SAQ, you don't just skip it, but that you have a go at it. Then we suggest that you compare what you have done with what we have said in our response to the SAQ. We suggest that you don't cheat yourself by reading on through the chapters without seeing what our responses are to the SAQs – in fact, most of the important points we offer are included in the responses and not just in the text of the book. We also urge you to resist the temptation to look at our responses before you've actually had a go at the questions. We can't respond to what you haven't done! Skipping ahead to the responses isn't actually a short cut for you – it's a way of short-changing yourself!

So how do we suggest you make the most of this book?

By using it actively, as we've already explained. But also, we suggest you use this book often – it's not the sort of book to use once then put on the shelf. Ideally, we would like this book to be a companion to your studies. For example, spending a few minutes with this book regularly can pay dividends. Different chapters will take on their own significance as your studies progress. Whatever you're studying, it's obviously important for you to get a grip on your subjects. However, we suggest that even more important is your mission to become a highly accomplished *learner*, and that's what we hope this book will help you to do. The skills you develop regarding your learning strategies will serve you for the whole of your future – long after subject knowledge has been overtaken by new developments.

A bird's eye view of the contents of the book

Chapter 1 'Why are you doing it?' essentially deals with the 'wanting' part of the learning process. We hope that by the end of this chapter, you'll have even stronger reasons for wanting to succeed with your studies.

Chapter 2 'What are the difficulties?' tackles some of the things that could get in the way of your want to learn. Being aware of any problems is the most important step in overcoming them.

Chapter 3 'What are your resources?' should be comforting and reassuring. It should help you enhance your want to learn. Moreover, it should give you further ideas about how you can put these resources into play and help ensure that the ways that you learn are powerful and successful.

Chapter 4 'How's your competence?' gives you a chance to make sense of (digest) the way that you learn. You'll find in this chapter that it's a really good thing every time you discover something you don't yet know but may need to know in due course.

Chapter 5 'When will you find the time?' is essentially about learning-by-doing – and making sure that you find enough time to do enough practising.

Chapter 6 'Where will you study?' aims to alert you to some work-avoidance strategies which may hinder your progress. Essentially, if you're really going to be an effective part-time student, you will be that wherever you are, and not just when you're sitting at your study-table or desk.

Chapter 7 'How can your make studying really efficient?' gets back to the importance of learning-by-doing, and finding the time to make sure that you get enough practising in.

Chapter 8 'How can active learning guarantee successful study?' aims to help you more with making sure that your learning is based on learning-by-doing and practising, and avoiding less-effective things such as passive reading.

Chapter 9 'How can you get the best from your tutors?' aims to help you make the most of learning from feedback. Tutors are human beings! If you use them in the most sensible ways, you'll get a lot more out of their feedback.

Chapter 10 'How can you find out how well you're doing?' is about finding out how you're getting on, and making sense of your learning. In terms of what we've said earlier about effective learning, this chapter should help you further with making use of feedback and 'digesting' the knowledge and information that you meet as you continue to learn.

Chapter 11 'How will you cope with revision and exams?' is particularly important in that it tends to be exam performance that is the final arbiter of the success of your learning. We don't actually think that exams are a good measure of people's capability! However, the best we can do is to help you make sure that in this particular game you are equipped to be a winner. When we look at exams in a cool and logical way, it boils down to deciding how best to use learning-by-doing to prepare to demonstrate what you can indeed do.

Chapter 12 'Staying the course' is the most philosophical chapter of our book. If you've picked up all the ideas and suggestions we've been hinting at in the earlier chapters, we believe you'll be ready to take charge of your own way of making sure that you 'stay the course' – and succeed.

Chapter 1

Why Are You Doing It?

Let's make sure that you have some good reasons. There'll be times when you'll need them.

It's a great strength to be clear about your reasons for studying. You're more likely to be successful if you are sure of your goal(s). Of course this goes for other activities in life too. When the going gets tough it's valuable to be able to keep up your motivation by reminding yourself of the reasons why you're doing your course. That's why we've included this chapter. When you've worked through it you'll have a clearer idea about what you can expect to get out of your course. In particular, you'll be more able to:

- feel a clear sense of purpose in what you're doing
- recite some good reasons for sticking to your studies with enough conviction to keep you at them even on those dark days that we all get from time to time.

People learn things for all sorts of reasons, some better than others. Let's go straight to your reasons. Have a go at the following SAQ.

SAQ 1.1

Why are you studying? What are your aims? What do you hope to get out of it? Choose which of the following 15 options particularly applies to you. Possibly more than one option fits your case. If so, tick each of the relevant ones. Then look at the back of the book for our comments on the options that you chose – and about the ones that you didn't.

I'm studying because:

1   I'm bored and I need a challenge
2   The topic I'm studying will be useful in my job

continued ↓

---

3   Mastering the topic could lead to promotion
4   Mastering the topic could lead to more choice in potential employment
5   Someone told me to study
6   I've always wanted to study this topic and now's my chance
7   I simply like learning new things
8   A friend or colleague studied it and recommended it
9   I want to prove to myself or others that I'm up to it
10   I want to be able to keep up with and help my children
11   To get an educational qualification for a higher-level course
12   To acquire more self-confidence
13   To broaden my horizons and develop my mind
14   To make up for missed educational opportunities in the past
15   I've got my own reasons. Write them down here to remind you what
     they are:

Now we've looked at a number of possible reasons for studying. There are probably as many different reasons as there are learners – and we're all learners! Don't worry that some of our responses to the options in SAQ 1.1 ended on something of a 'warning note': we wanted to get you thinking about how many of your reasons for learning would stand up to pressure. You'll have seen from our responses to the options you chose in SAQ 1.1 how well your reasons are going to serve you. You may even have found some new and better reasons for studying. If so, we're glad.

SAQ 1.2

Some time ago we carried out a study of the educational experiences of students enrolled on part-time degree courses in higher education.[1] We sent a questionnaire out to over 4000 part-time students and received replies from about 70 per cent of them. One of the questions contained a list of possible aims and the students were invited to indicate how important each was in their decision to enrol. In the light of our discussion of reasons for learning you might like to try the same questionnaire now and compare your answers with the replies that we got from the part-time undergraduates.

(A)   When you decided to enrol for your course what did you hope to get out of it? Please read through the aims listed below and indicate for each one how important it was in your decision.

(Please ring one number for each aim shown below)

Table 1.1 *Aims*

	Very important	Fairly important	Not important
Work-related aims			
To improve my career prospects:	1	2	3
To improve my chance of promotion/ increased salary in my present type of work:	1	2	3
To increase the opportunities for changing my job:	1	2	3
To help me do my present job better:	1	2	3
Subject-related aims			
To learn more about a subject that interests me:	1	2	3
To get an educational qualification for a higher-level course:	1	2	3
To develop a shared interest with my spouse/partner, friend, etc:	1	2	3

continued ↓

Table 1.1 *Aims (continued)*	Very important	Fairly important	Not important
Personal development aims			
To prove to myself (or others) that I could complete a degree course:	1	2	3
To widen my horizons:	1	2	3
To develop my mind:	1	2	3
To acquire more self-confidence:	1	2	3
General aims			
To make up for lack of educational opportunities in the past:	1	2	3
To benefit my children's education:	1	2	3
To get away from my usual surroundings and responsibilities at home:	1	2	3
To make new friends with similar interests:	1	2	3

(B) Which one of these aims would you say was most important in your case?

You've now had another opportunity to explore your motives for doing your course. We've laboured this a bit and for a good purpose. We need good reasons for doing demanding things like studying. The more reasons the better. When things get hard, these reasons can be the driving force that keeps us on course. Let's face it, it's bound to be tough now and then – things that are worthwhile usually are. Imagine if higher education institutes gave all students a degree certificate no matter how little they worked. A degree would be quite worthless. There wouldn't be any point in working for one.

Activity

In SAQ 1.1 you found a list of possible 'reasons' for doing a part-time course of study and in SAQ 1.2 you will have found a list of 'aims'. You'll see that there's a lot of overlap between these reasons and aims. Now review both lists and after identifying the ones that apply to you, rank them in terms of how important they are to you:

- My most important reason is ...

- My second most important reason is ...

- My third most important reason is ...

Another activity

Ask others on your course why they are doing it and compare your reasons with them.

Ultimately, the only person who can assess how good your reasons are for learning is yourself. That's why we're not going to say any more. If we've helped you to reappraise your motives, well and good.

We hope that you've now got a clearer sense of the reasons for what you're doing. We hope that these will sustain you on those dark days that we all get from time to time so that you're more likely to stay the course.

Note

1 A full report of this research was published as *Part-time Undergraduates and their Experience of Higher Education* by the Open University Press in 1991.

Chapter 2

What Are The Difficulties?

We've looked at reasons for undertaking a course of part-time study. Practical positive thinking. In this chapter we'll do some practical negative thinking. We'll tackle the difficulties that confront part-time students. Students who are winners spend time anticipating difficulties that they might encounter in successfully completing their course. Forewarned is forearmed. If you know what the possible obstacles are then you're more able to deal successfully with them.

When you've studied this chapter you'll be clearer about:

- what pitfalls are most often encountered by part-time students
- which of the potential pitfalls are likely to apply to you in particular
- what steps you can take to avoid some of the most common pitfalls.

Potential pitfalls

If you haven't sorted out in your own mind what difficulties you are likely to face then you're not in a position to plan how to handle them. Sometimes we've got vague anxieties or concerns about a course of action but we're not completely clear about what they are. SAQ 2.1 will help you to sort out the obstacles that you might face.

SAQ 2.1

Which of the following items do you feel are likely to be a difficulty for you? Put a tick against the ones that you choose.

Study and learning difficulties
- Keeping up with the academic level of the course
- Finding the time to study
- Being able to grasp the meaning of specialised terms and concepts

---

- Organising my time in an efficient way
- Developing confidence in my academic ability
- Remembering important parts of my course
- Coming to terms with the academic way of looking at things
- Developing appropriate study skills (eg writing essays)
- Coping with the stress of examinations
- Getting used to the college environment
- Getting used to a different approach to learning
- Getting used to a subject never previously studied.

Personal, family and job commitments
- Coping with family commitments
- Coping with job demands
- Coping with the financial costs of the course
- Coping with competing demands of hobbies and other interests
- Making friends with fellow students
- Coming to terms with changing values, beliefs and attitudes
- Coping with travel to and from college.

Now, for the ones that you've ticked, write a number beside each tick as follows:

1   I expect this to be a *significant* difficulty for me.
2   I expect this to be a *substantial* difficulty for me.
3   I expect this to be a *major* difficulty for me.

And now have a look at *our* responses at the back of the book.

Finding the time

In our response to SAQ 2.1, using information from our researches we looked at the unexpected difficulties that part-time students encounter. What makes this a particularly key issue is a result from a follow-up study that we did a year later into the subsequent progress of the students in the sample. We found that the drop-out rate for those students who had said that 'the difficulties overall were greater than I expected when I decided to enrol' were about two-thirds higher than for the others. Top of the list of unexpected difficulties from our survey came 'finding the time to study'. The next four were 'coping with competing demands of hobbies and other interests', 'organising my time in an efficient way', 'coping with job demands' and 'coping with family commitments'. So problems with time management were probably present in all of the top five difficulties.

Time management really means self-management. Especially if you're a mature student with family responsibilities and work commitments you're likely to find that managing your life becomes a bigger problem (a bigger challenge?) when you start a part-time course. As well as coping with your family and your job you now have to manage your course!

We don't mean to be discouraging. We *do* mean you to be realistic. There are at least half a million people in the United Kingdom enrolled on courses of part-time further and higher education. And the number is rising. So it clearly is possible to cope. The successful part-time students are the ones who think out in advance the likely difficulties and how they can handle them. You're already on your way to cracking the difficulties – after all, you're looking at this book.

Activity

If you haven't yet started your part-time course try this exercise. You'll probably find it handy to have a piece of paper and something to write with for this.

Estimate (roughly) how many hours you'll spend on your studies each week: include time spent studying (in classes and outside classes), time spent travelling to and from college (if applicable) and libraries, time spent drinking coffee with other students, etc. You don't have to be exact for this to be a useful exercise. Your 'estimate' of how much time you will spend on private study may well be more of a guess! No matter.

Now think about how you spend your time in a 'typical' week. If you don't have a typical week that doesn't matter either, just think back to last week.

Now think about how you'll fit in the extra hours associated with doing your part-time course. Which activities in your week are you prepared to sacrifice? Which ones are you prepared to do less of? Try to be realistic. If you currently come home each night and crash out in front of the television for a few hours then it's pretty unrealistic to say that you'll stop watching television altogether. You may, however, decide to watch less television and you may decide to get clear what programmes you are going to give priority to. In fact, the value of this exercise lies in helping you to sort out your priorities in how you use your time.

Sorting out when you'll find the time to study is clearly a key part of winning as a part-time student. That's why we've devoted the whole of Chapter 5 to it.

Forethought and preparation clearly help. For this it pays to look at the difficulties encountered by other part-time students. That way you can reduce the number of unexpected difficulties that come your way. Learning from the errors of others is less painful than learning from your own errors! However, since you're a unique person (there's no one else quite like you in the universe) you're likely to find your own special difficulties. And since you're not gifted with perfect foresight you may not anticipate them all. So can you do anything to prepare yourself for difficulties that you can't even predict? Yes, you can do the next activity...

Another activity

If you're going to manage the extra demands of taking on a part-time course successfully, then you'll probably benefit from some help. The fact that you're working through this book suggests that you're smart enough to realise that.

It will be easier to manage the demands if you've created a supportive context for yourself. Have a talk with the significant others in your life who can make things easier or more difficult for you. Talk over why the course is important to you – the reasons that you're taking it. Talk over what it's likely to mean in terms of your commitment in effort, time and money. Who are the 'significant others' who can make life easier or more difficult for you? Only you can know for sure but you might consider any of the following list:

- your spouse/partner/girlfriend/boyfriend
- other members of your family
- friends outside work
- people who you work with
- your employer or boss

continued ↓

- college staff
- fellow students.

By working through this book you're less likely to be 'sandbagged' by unexpected difficulties. But no matter how well prepared, you may still encounter some unexpected obstacles. If you have developed the understanding and support of those who are important to you then you'll have done much to surmount the hurdles that you encounter. The rest of this book has got suggestions for dealing with other pitfalls. As you work through the book you'll find ideas for handling the more common difficulties that part-time students experience.

Checklist

Now that you've explored the things that cause most difficulty to part-time students, are you more aware of:

- the unexpected pitfalls most often encountered?
- the potential pitfalls which are most likely to apply to you in particular?
- some steps that you can take to avoid the most common pitfalls?

Chapter 3 looks at the weapons in your armoury to deal with the problems and pitfalls you have identified by going through this chapter.

Chapter 3

What Are Your Resources?

In this chapter we'll look at the resources you need to help you win. The chapter was written in the belief that you've already got more of these resources than you realise and that you can develop others. If you marshall your resources well then you raise the odds on being successful.

When you've worked through this chapter you should:

- be able to list a wide range of potential resources for successfully completing a part-time course of study
- be able to identify which of your potential resources are currently available to you
- be aware of ways of turning your potential resources into actual resources
- have an action plan to increase the range and depth of resources for successfully completing your part-time course.

Potential resources

We think that you've already got more resources to help you to be successful on your part-time course than you realise. Try SAQ 3.1 and find out if this is true.

SAQ 3.1

Make a list of all the resources that you've got to help you to successfully complete your part-time course (see if you can identify at least 20):

continued ↓

Activity

Some of the items on the list in our response to SAQ 3.1 will be useful resources to you, others may not be. Spend a few minutes adding items from our list that you feel might be particularly useful to you. When you've done this give your list a star rating – 3 stars for 'really powerful' resources, 2 for 'useful ones' and 1 for 'quite useful' ones.

You'll see from our response to SAQ 3.1 that we've classified resources into 'people' and 'things'. Our experience is that other people are a key source of resources. It's important to develop a network of people who can provide you with different kinds of support. Later on in this chapter we'll consider who might be worth including in your support network and how you can go about developing and enhancing such a network.

College resources

Are you aware that every office and service at your college exists to help you to successfully complete your course? This may seem obvious in the case of, say, the college library, but not so obvious in the case of, say, the departmental office of the department in which your course is located. At some colleges these offices and services are actually called support services. In the final analysis they're there to support *you* – either directly or indirectly. It will pay you to find out about them so that you can make the most of them. Otherwise don't blame others if you don't get all the value out of them that you could.

SAQ 3.2

We said that you're probably not aware of all the resources available to you. That goes for the resources available to you from your college too. Spend a few minutes making a list of all the support services available from your college and then compare your list with our response to SAQ 3.2.

When you start your course you'll probably get more information about it and your college than you can absorb. Much of it will slip by you. So a good strategy is to spend some time *before you start your course* finding out about the resources that your college has to offer. Even if you're an 'evening-only' student why not take an afternoon off work and explore your new college? You might also make a note of the location of the telephones and the nearest pub. Apart from the value of this information as a resource it will also help you to feel more comfortable more quickly. Then you can pay more attention to your classes.

This would be equally worthwhile for students who aren't so new: it's most unlikely that you know all that is worth knowing about what your college can provide. Find out why the offices, services and other facilities exist and how to get most value from them. Be assertive. It pays to make personal contact with the people who run the place. You may be surprised how well these people respond when you take an interest in what they do and the contribution that they make to the place.

Activity

Using our response to SAQ 3.2, tick off eight places in your college to find out more about and write down several questions for each that you'd like answers to. If you feel shy about this see if you can find a partner – another student on your course – to do it with. That way you'll also be developing a friend on the course – a double pay-off.

Most part-time students stress the importance of their fellow students in their success. Fellow students are there to swap ideas with. They can give you feedback on how you're doing. They can collect handouts for you the week that you miss because of a family emergency. You can check things out with them that you didn't understand at a lecture. They can share their resources (they might have particularly easy access to photocopying facilities for example). They can proof-read an essay or report for you (presumably on a reciprocal basis!). Most of all they are your comrades in adversity: a support group who understand better than anyone the concerns that you may have about the course. It's worth spending time and effort getting to know at least some of your fellow students very well indeed!

It's also worth getting to know some of the students in the year ahead of you. They are a source of tangible benefits such as cheap used copies of textbooks. They are also in a position to share with you their experience of what your year of the course is really like – the pitfalls and the bits to look forward to. Our experience is that most part-time students will be pleased to share their experience with someone following in their footsteps.

Home resources

We've already stressed the importance of developing support at home. In our research we got responses from almost 2900 part-time undergraduates to the question: 'How encouraging or discouraging are the following people about you taking your course?' In working out the results we eliminated the 'not applicable' responses.

Table 3.1 *Encouragement from others*

	Very supportive %	Generally supportive %	Neutral/ no effect %	Discouraging or opposed %
Spouse/partner:	63	28	5	3[†]
Other members of your family:	37	41	21	2[†]
Friends outside work:	11	35	52	2
People who work with you:	16	45	34	4[†]
Your employer:	27	41	27	5
College staff:	34	53	13	0[*]
Fellow students:	33	48	18	0[*†]

*   Less than 0.5 per cent.

†   Owing to rounding, not all horizontal percentages sum to precisely 100.

It's clear from this table that the students got little discouragement from any of the sources. They got most encouragement from their families – especially from their partners. Next in terms of encouragement came other members of their course – staff and fellow students. Work (employers and work friends) provided a supportive context for about two-thirds of the sample. For a majority of the respondents, friends outside work were seen as having a neutral impact on their motivation.

It's likely that the results shown in the table reflect the sources of encouragement actually sought by the students. Most married students, for example, are presumably aware of the need to secure the support of their spouse in view of the impact of undertaking part-time study on domestic arrangements and responsibilities. What steps can you take to widen the base of your support to include less obvious people who are influential in your life such as friends outside work?

Work resources

You may or may not be in paid employment at the moment. If you are, then this section is for you. Your place of work can be a source of additional pressures and responsibilities. It can also be a source of significant resources. Remember that in our response to SAQ 3.1 there was a section headed work resources. It included the following items:

- the boss
- work colleagues
- finance
- work library resources
- photocopiers
- typing facilities
- equipment.

We saw in Table 3.1 that the people that you work with can be a useful source of support. Your employer is likely to be supportive if only because when you increase your abilities by completing your part-time course he or she is likely to benefit. Some employers are positively enthusiastic.

To quote our research findings again: 95 per cent of our respondents who were in current paid employment reported that their employers (or supervisors) were aware that they were taking their part-time course. Of these, the large majority received some kind of financial support. The majority also received support in some other way(s):

Table 3.2 *Workplace support*

	% of respondents in current paid employment who received employer support
Employer pays or refunds the whole of the fees	65
Pays or refunds part of the fees	15

	%
Travelling allowance	38
Book and/or equipment allowance	26
Time off to attend classes with pay	51
Time off to attend classes without pay	6
Additional study leave (eg before exams)	36
Reduced workload	4
Use of the employer's facilities (eg library, laboratory, computer)	34

You can see from the table that about 80 per cent of those in current paid employment received at least some help with their fees from their employers. In general, this table gives the impression of a supportive attitude by employers. After all, it's in their own interest to be supportive. So don't assume that your employer won't help. Let your employer know what you are doing. And ask for the help that you need.

Personal resources

Sometimes it can seem that full-time students have all the advantages: time, freedom from responsibilities, etc. Certainly they've got more time. That's why we focused on the issue in the previous chapter. Freedom from responsibilities is another matter. Can you remember what it was like when you were a teenager, coping with love and your own sexuality for the first time? Can you remember how vitally important other people's opinions of you seemed? Perhaps it's just that your worries now are different from what they were then. Perhaps with your greater maturity other people's opinions don't seem quite so important now. Perhaps your resources are different now from what they were then.

SAQ 3.3

Think back to when you left school. What can you now do that you couldn't do then? You'll have increased your stock of some personal resources and decreased your stock of others. Put a tick against any of the following that you have more of now than you had then:

- technical skills

continued ↓

- conceptual skills
- social skills
- organisational skills
- commitment/motivation to complete course
- money
- self-confidence
- intelligence
- energy
- information
- support from others
- study skills
- time.

Please do this SAQ carefully. It's worth it because you'll get more value from our response if you do. We've responded at length to this SAQ.

Were you surprised by parts of our response to SAQ 3.3? Did you realise that you have so many resources to compensate for the reduced time available to you? We want to explore this theme further with you. We'll do so by means of another SAQ. SAQ 3.4 is on the same lines as the previous one but this time we'll look in more detail at the skills that you have developed since you have left school. It will help you to take stock of this part of your resources.

SAQ 3.4 Skills inventory

This SAQ is like the last one. Here we want you to take stock of the specific conceptual, technical and social skills that you have developed. Put a tick against all the skills in the following skills inventory that you have more of now than you had when you left school. You'll see that it's a long list but you'll be able to work through it quickly as you've only got to tick items in the list.

Conceptual skills
- Applying judgement
- Visualising things as they could be rather than accepting the status quo
- Reviewing large amounts of material and extracting the essence

SAQ 3.4 *continued*

- Perceiving and defining 'cause and effect' relationships
- Tracing problems and ideas to their source
- Conceiving, developing and generating creative or original ideas
- Setting goals
- Extrapolating from the known to the unknown
- Formulating policy on the basis of identified goals
- Synthesising information from different sources
- Seeing relationships between apparently unrelated factors
- Thinking laterally
- Problem-solving
- Integrating different opinions or viewpoints
- Seeing a theoretical base in practical situations
- Breaking down an issue into its key components
- Recognising the need for more information before a good decision can be made
- Thinking logically
- Organising written material
- Evaluating different views
- Analysing quantitative information
- Analysing qualitative information
- Ability to interpret different views
- Ability to suspend judgement
- Designing projects
- Showing careful attention to detail
- Taking a broad perspective
- Planning: breaking work into manageable chunks that fit together effectively
- Scheduling: determining when and in what order things should be done in a project to minimise crises and wasted efforts
- Monitoring: keeping track of what tasks have been completed
- Reviewing: establishing what targets are/are not being met, where problems are emerging and identifying possible needs to redirect resources
- Evaluating: stepping back to take stock of how well arrangements are meeting targets, whether the right methods are being used and whether the right targets are being tackled.

continued ↓

SAQ 3.4 *continued*

Technical skills
- Driving a car or motorcycle
- Repairing/maintaining a car or motorcycle
- Using a computer
- Writing computer programs
- Typing
- Word processing
- Presenting data visually
- Using specialised planning techniques (such as critical path analysis)
- Using foreign language(s):
    - reading
    - writing
    - translating
    - conversation
    - interpreting technical/business talk
- Working with laboratory equipment
- Working with machines or technical equipment
- Estimating what resources a project will need and in what quantities
- Accounting and/or bookkeeping
- Planning systems and procedures
- Appraising investment
- Preparing written materials
- Preparing transparencies for overhead projectors
- Designing
- Preparing documentation for computer systems
- Preparing and writing reports
- Editing
- Applying what others have done
- Preparing, controlling and reviewing projects
- Analysing performance specifications
- Taking photographs
- Making videos or shooting films
- Making cassette recordings
- Gathering information

SAQ 3.4 *continued*

- Illustrating
- Cartooning
- Setting up monitoring systems on tasks and uses of resources and controlling through corrective action
- Developing written questionnaires.

Social skills

- Assessing the skills and resources of others
- Assessing the potential performance of others
- Making and using contacts effectively
- Encouraging people
- Sharing enthusiasm
- Getting diverse groups to work together
- Inspiring trust
- Developing rapport with others
- Helping others to identify their own self-interest
- Influencing the attitudes or ideas of others
- Developing a line of thought persuasively
- Identifying sponsors
- Enlisting the support of others
- Awareness of political (small p) factors
- Asserting clearly your own wants and requirements from a particular situation
- Mediating between contending parties or groups
- Non-verbal communication
- Negotiating with others (eg clarifying objectives of all parties and exploring alternative options)
- Responding sensitively to the mood of listeners
- Making presentations
- Addressing large groups
- Pinpointing clearly the information that is needed by individuals or groups and how to communicate it economically in ways that will be received
- Expressing yourself well verbally
- Writing concisely and to the point

continued ↓

SAQ 3.4 *continued*

- Instructing/teaching/training
- Confronting others with touchy or difficult personal matters
- Fostering willingness to work
- Catalysing a team – getting people going, energising them, holding their interest
- Dealing with controversy
- Presenting an argument
- Handling 'difficult' people
- Listening to others attentively and accurately
- Communicating warmth, understanding and patience to others
- Briefing others
- Explaining clearly
- Delegating
- Interpreting others' attitudes and motives
- Assessing and evaluating the performance of others
- Using humour to encourage and interest others
- Creating an atmosphere of acceptance and self-acceptance
- Chairing meetings
- Facilitating groups
- Representing others
- Assessing the needs of others
- Interviewing (in person)
- Interviewing (on the phone)
- Resolving difficulties between people
- Counselling
- Giving feedback
- Accepting feedback
- Networking
- Building on the ideas of others
- Servicing the human needs of others by organising facilities (eg arranging rooms, dates of meetings, access to coffee/tea, etc)
- Maintaining a group or team – keeping it going after the initial enthusiasm has worn off
- Initiating change
- Making 'cold' speculative approaches to potential contacts:
    - by letter

SAQ 3.4 *continued*

  - – by phone
  - – in person
- Liaising between technical specialists
- Organising events (eg displays, exhibitions, seminars, plays, trips).

(Phew – what a long SAQ!)

So now you know you've got a lot more resources by way of skills than you realised. Let's backtrack to that discussion of intelligence and age in our response to SAQ 3.3. The sort of intelligence that we had in mind was the sort of analytical intelligence that is measured in IQ tests. In fact, this is only one sort of intelligence. Howard Gardner at Harvard University's Graduate School of Education has identified seven different types of intelligence. According to Gardner they are separately measurable and not highly correlated. Charles Handy, in his book *The Age of Unreason* (Hutchinson, 1989), gave a simplified account of these as follows:

1   *Analytical intelligence* – the sort we measure in IQ tests.
2   *Pattern intelligence* – the ability to see pattern relationships in things.
     Mathematicians, artists, computer programmers often have this
     type of intelligence to a high degree.
3   *Practical intelligence* – people with this sort of intelligence can take car
     engines to bits and put them back together again without
     instructions and without having any parts left over at the end!
4   *Musical intelligence* – many musicians, including musicians in pop
     bands, have a good helping of analytical intelligence. Many have
     not.
5   *Physical intelligence* – boxers, gymnasts, footballers and sporting stars
     of all types have this sort of intelligence.
6   *Intrapersonal intelligence* – people with this sort of intelligence are in
     touch with their feelings.
7   *Interpersonal intelligence* – this sort of intelligence enables people to
     pick up social skills with ease. People who are well endowed with
     interpersonal intelligence get on well with others and find it easy
     to get things done with and through others.

All of these types of intelligence, in the right context, can be of value to someone doing a part-time course. Just how valuable depends on the specific nature of the course. For example, pattern intelligence would be a great asset if you're doing a part-time maths degree, and intrapersonal intelligence would be a particular asset if you're doing a course in counselling or poetry appreciation.

There is increasing if belated recognition of the value of these different types of intelligence. To quote Handy:

> The new 16+ examination recognises that there is more to learning than memorising and analytical intelligence. It is, at last, a formal acknowledgement that problem-solving is at the heart of learning and therefore to be welcomed as one step towards a better future. The Records of Achievement used in many schools are a way of acknowledging achievement in the other intelligences. (p 176)

SAQ 3.5

Have another look at the seven types of intelligence identified above and tick the four you think you score most highly at.

> *Analytical intelligence*
> *Pattern intelligence*
> *Practical intelligence*
> *Musical intelligence*
> *Physical intelligence*
> *Intrapersonal intelligence*
> *Interpersonal intelligence.*

Now rank the ones that you've ticked by placing 1 against the type of intelligence with which you are most endowed, 2 against your next strongest and so on.

Developing your resources

So far in this chapter we've emphasised becoming more aware of the potential resources that you already have. We've stressed the word 'potential' for a purpose. Some of your potential resources will already be available to you. These will not only be potential resources, they'll also be *actual* resources. You'll need to work on some of the other potential resources, however, to turn them into actual resources that are available to you.

We've emphasised the importance of other people as a resource to you. It's through other people that you're likely to get access to most of the resources that we put in the 'things' category in our response to SAQ 3.1. In addition, other people can directly provide you with two essential resources: support and feedback. It's important to set up a support network to help you cope with the times when your enthusiasm wanes and you energy levels are low.

SAQ 3.6

Can you identify a support network and the kinds of support provided by the people in your support network? In the spaces provided write in the names of people who provide you with different kinds of support. In the last column on the right of the page place a tick if you feel that you don't get a certain type of support and consider possible reasons for it.

Table 3.3 *Types of support*

	At work	Away from work	If I don't get this support at all, why don't I?
Someone I can always rely on			
Someone I just enjoy chatting with			
Someone with whom I've discussed things I've done on the course			
Someone who makes me feel competent and valued			
Someone who gives me constructive feedback			

continued ↓

Table 3.3 *continued*

	At work	Away from work	If I don't get this support at all, why don't I?
Someone who is a good source of information			
Someone I can depend upon in a crisis			
Someone I can feel close to – a friend or intimate			
Someone I can share bad news with			
Someone I can share good news and good feelings with			
Someone who introduces me to new ideas, new interests, new people			

An action plan

Do you need to increase the range and depth of resources to successfully complete your course? What specific steps can you take? First, identify which of your potential resources are currently available to you. You'll find it useful to turn to the results of the brainstorm that we showed in our response to SAQ 3.1. Use this as a checklist. What can you do to make sure that the items that you see here as potentially valuable resources will be available as actual resources when you need them? Do you want to join another library? Do you want to get hold of a copy of last year's exam paper? What specific actions can you take? Don't let these 'actions' remain as just good intentions – do something about them.

The first thing that you can do is to complete the following action plan.

Things I'm going to do or find out about	How I'm going to go about it	When I'm going to do it
•		
•		
•		
•		
•		
•		
•		
•		

Checklist

In this chapter we've looked at the resources available to you to help you win. Now that you've worked through it we hope that:

- you're aware of a wider range of potential resources for successfully completing a part-time course of study

- you can identify which of your potential resources are currently available to you

- you've thought about ways of turning your potential resources into actual resources

- you have an action plan to increase the range and depth of resources.

We also hope that knowing all the resources that are available to you – potential and actual – gives you more confidence that you will be successful.

Chapter 4

How's Your Competence?
(Modern equivalent of 'first, know thyself'!)

In the last chapter we looked at resources – and we hope you were pleasantly surprised by how many resources you can make use of. In the present chapter we'll be exploring one major resource that we know you've got – the resources of your mind. Our purpose in this chapter is to help you give yourself a confidence boost and to help you to work out how best to put the ideas in this book to work for you. It's been said that the single most important factor in guaranteeing success in studying is confidence. There's nothing like finding out how competent you really are for helping you be more confident.

What's competence?

'Competence' is a word that has been with us for a long time – and a word we hear a lot about today. Increasingly, the things you need to learn to gain qualifications are being expressed in 'competence statements'. It's always being said 'we need competent graduates, not just knowledgeable ones'. So there's a difference between being knowledgeable and being competent. But do we know what competence means? Try SAQ 4.1.

SAQ 4.1

Think of someone you know who is competent. Jot down his or her name (if you're sure that the person concerned will not read what follows!), then write down a few things that are evidence for him or her being competent.

Name:

Evidence for competence:

-
-

continued ↓

-
-

(You may like to show it to the person concerned anyway. If so, check what he or she regards as evidence for competence too.)

The opposite of competence?

Now that we've got a model of competence (as you saw in our response to SAQ 4.1), let's think about the opposite of competence. We'll not ask you to write down the name of a person who isn't competent, and list evidence to support your assertion – that could be dangerous! (Go on, do it if you must, but not in this book!) Instead let's keep it general – try SAQ 4.2, it couldn't be shorter!!

SAQ 4.2

What's the opposite of competence? And how could this be recognised?

People and their competences

We started off by thinking of a 'competent' person, but in fact the only way to be objective about it is to think of competences and uncompetences. (If that last word threw you, you didn't read our response to SAQ 4.2!)

In reality, each of us has all sorts of things we can do (competences) and all sorts of things we can't do – or don't need to do – or don't want to do – or won't do (all 'uncompetences' as defined in our response to SAQ 4.2). So perhaps our quest shouldn't just be to become 'competent people', but to develop those *particular* competences which we need for whatever is our purpose or ambition.

We've now looked at the meaning of competence – and its opposite. But do we always know what our own competences and uncompetences are? Do we always know specifically what competences we're going to need? The fact is we don't always know this. The more we can do to find out the better our chances at being successful when preparing for competence to be tested.

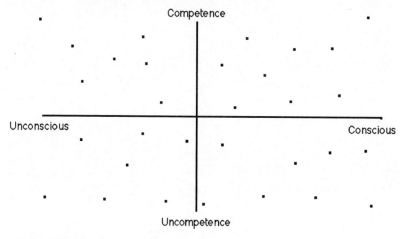

Figure 4.1 *The four boxes*

Conscious and unconscious competence and uncompetence

Think of it like a map as shown in Figure 4.1. There are four 'boxes' on this map, and each of us has all sorts of things in each box. That's why we've spattered points all over. In fact, we're talking about a three-dimensional set – the missing dimension is time. Figure 4.1 is just a cross-section showing the present time. Let's look at each box in turn.

The axes on Figure 4.1 are of course quite arbitrary. It's hard to say where uncompetence ends and competence begins – just as it's hard to say where unconsciousness ends and consciousness begins. However, we think that from your own experience you'll be able to relate to things that lie in each of the four boxes. Please read on.

Conscious competence – the target box

This is the box where not only you *can do* things, but you *know* you can do them. This is the ideal situation to be in with each of your subjects when going in for an exam – that's one reason why we called it the target box. You'll already have all sorts of things in this box, relevant not just to studying but to life in general.

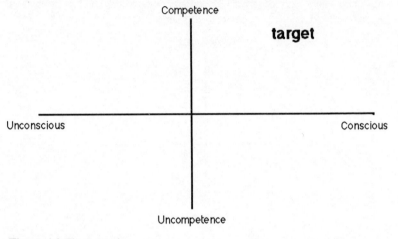

Figure 4.2 *The target box*

Take a few minutes to map out things you have in this box – try SAQ 4.3.

SAQ 4.3

Jot down half a dozen things you can do – and you know you can do – things you're confident about. Don't be modest! The things can be about anything at all, not just studying.

Conscious uncompetence – the transit box
Conscious uncompetence we've defined as things you *know* you:

- can't *yet* do
- don't *want* to do
- don't *need* to do
- *won't* do

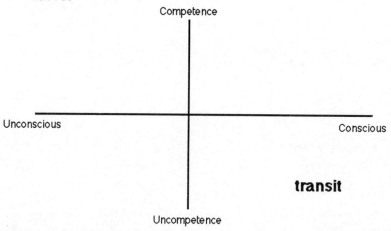

Figure 4.3 *The transit box*

Most of the things in this box are perfectly all right where they are. There may be no point doing anything about the things you don't *need* to do. There may be no need to develop competences that you don't *want* to do. It's probably ill-advised to try to develop competences you feel you *won't* do. So there's only 'can't *yet* do' left to think about.

We called this the *transit* box because once you've identified things that you can't yet do you're well on the way to becoming able to do them! The real problem is *not knowing* what you can't yet do. But that's another box – more about that soon. Try SAQ 4.4 now.

SAQ 4.4

Jot down a few things that belong in your *conscious uncompetence* box. Try to include things under each of these subheadings:

- can't *yet* do

- don't *want* to do

- don't *need* to do

- *won't* do

Unconscious uncompetence – the danger box!
We've already asked you to jot down some of your conscious competences and your conscious uncompetences. That was straightforward enough. But what if we were to ask you to jot down some of your unconscious uncompetences? You can't – or at least you shouldn't be able to!

But let us ask you another question: do you know someone who is unconsciously uncompetent at something or other? Almost certainly: we can imagine you smiling as you think of such a person! There are plenty of such people around. By implication, we are also going to have unconscious uncompetences – but of course we don't know exactly what they are. That's why we're calling this box the *danger* box – it contains things that we *don't know we can't yet do.*

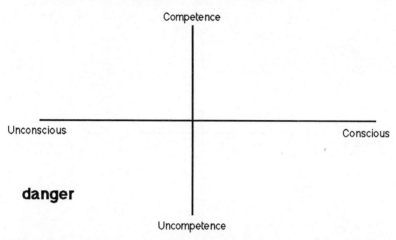

Figure 4.4 *The danger box*

This box will also contain things we *don't know we don't want to do*, and things we *don't know we don't need to do,* and even things we *don't know we won't do* – but none of these matter. These unconscious uncompetences are fine where they are – no need to do anything about them. However, the things that *we don't know we can't yet do* could be a serious problem. Let's go further into this.

Imagine you're about to go into an exam room. Soon you'll see the questions. As soon as you see them, you wish you'd revised all sorts of things that you haven't revised. The problem: you didn't know what you didn't know – until you saw the questions! This is quite some problem, but one with well-tested solutions which we'll address in several chapters of this book. Meanwhile, let's leave it as being a good idea to be constantly *finding out* exactly what you *can't yet do* – well before you *need* to prove that you can do it!

Unconscious competence – the magic box
This is the last of our four boxes, and you have lots of things in it. Again of course, you can't tell us what those things are – if you could they'd be in the conscious competence box. But there are ways of finding out what your unconscious competences are – the things you didn't realise that you *can do.* It's a great feeling

every time you discover one of these unconscious competences – that's why we've called this the *magic* box.

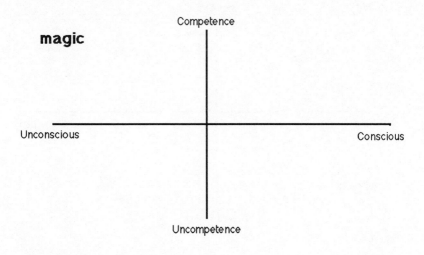

Figure 4.5 *The magic box*

You may not be able to spot your own unconscious competences, but other people can often help you discover them. Similarly, you will often be able to see other people's unconscious competences. Let's try an example.

SAQ 4.5

Jenny has an office job – not a very interesting one. She's going back to studying so that she can get more qualifications so she can get a job she really will enjoy. She has two children, both at school now (she took a few years away from work when they were younger). She's lucky in that her husband is very supportive of her wishes to study, and helps a lot with things at home. Jenny, however, is quite apprehensive about whether she'll be able to cope with keeping the home going, keeping her present job, and studying. Can you think of some unconscious competences she may not know she has?

How will your competence be measured?

Sooner or later the day of reckoning comes – your competence is to be assessed. It can take many forms:

- exams
- assignments
- projects
- interviews
- presentations you're asked to give

and so on.

All of these are situations where what you *can do* is being measured in one way or another. Or is it? In fact it's a bit more complex than that. What's measured is what you *do do* – not necessarily what you can do. See the difference?

How often have you thought (for example after an exam) 'I could have done much better'? In other words, what you did do wasn't as good as what you could do.

The problem is that no one has invented a computer or machine that you can be plugged into, that churns out a printout of what you *can do!* So, no one can really measure exactly what you *can do*. No one can measure your competence as such. What *is* measured is evidence of your competence. Or, putting it unkindly, if things go wrong what is measured is evidence of your lack of competence! That evidence takes many forms, such as the answers you give to exam questions, the performance you give at an interview, and so on.

What we're getting round to saying is that it's no use you having a lot of competence, if you can't produce the evidence of it in a form which will do you justice. Many of the ideas in the rest of this book are to help you do exactly this.

SWOT analysis

You may have heard of 'SWOT analysis'. You may already have tried it. Let's explain it in case it's new to you.

SWOT stands for four words:

- strengths
- weaknesses

- opportunities
- threats.

We're sure you'll agree that you have all four related to your task of being a part-time student.

SWOT analysis can be employed for all sorts of situations: you could do a SWOT analysis as a way of deciding whether to move house, or even to decide whether to get married. However, it's more often used regarding the planning of some new venture in work situations – and it lends itself very well to an analysis of the new venture of becoming a part-time student.

So, let's limit the analysis to things which relate closely to your situation as a part-time student. Shortly we'll ask you to write in things under each of the four headings, from your perspective as a part-time student. First though, let us explain a little more about the meanings you can give to the four terms.

Strengths: things you know you're good at which will help you as a part-time student. You may already have been thinking of some of these as conscious competences.

Weaknesses: things you know you're not good at – not yet that is. Many of these won't matter – they won't affect your being a part-time student. (We've already met something similar under the heading of conscious uncompetence – things you can't *yet* do.)

Opportunities: this is not directly to do with present 'can do' things (or 'can't yet do' things). It's to do with your answer to the question 'What's in it for me, as a *successful* part-time student?' It's to do with doors opening in your life. It's to do with chances you wouldn't have got if you hadn't taken up your studies.

Threats: probably the most direct way to look at these is to ask yourself 'What could stop me?' 'What could damage my motivation?' You may even need to address 'Who could stop me?' or 'How could I let myself down?'

We've said enough – it's time for you to have a go. Try SAQ 4.6.

SAQ 4.6

Spend some time being as objective as you can, filling things into the four boxes below. Try to stick to things that have a bearing on your studying. Look back at the explanations we gave about each of the four headings if this helps you.

Strengths | **Weaknesses**

Threats | **Opportunities**

Figure 4.6 *SWOT analysis*

Sharing with other people

Now that you've had a go at a SWOT analysis – and analysed your analysis along the lines we suggested in our response to SAQ 4.6 – we hope that you're feeling ready to get stuck into the rest of this book, and find out how to maximise your opportunities and strengths, minimise your threats, overcome any weaknesses, and develop those competences you need. *And* make sure you're going to be able to furnish exactly the right sort of *evidence* that's needed when the time comes to do so.

We hinted that it can be useful to bring other people into your confidence. For example, other people who know you can tell you a lot about your strengths (this feels good). What's more, people who know you can tell you things you didn't know – your unconscious competences (this feels even better). If such people are studying too, you can do the same for them (this makes them feel good). The start of a wonderful relationship perhaps!

But seriously, bringing other people into your confidence can have other benefits. People who know you can tell you about your weaknesses (this doesn't feel that good, but it's very useful to you). They can often tell you about your unconscious uncompetences (this doesn't feel good either, but it may be even more valuable to you).

There are opportunities to be gained by bringing other people into your confidence. It means that they're not being excluded from the world of your studies and this means that they're much more able to help when you need support. Also, if you are helping other part-time students with their plans, you're able to learn useful things simply by helping them overcome problems, and talking about issues that concern both them and you.

Not everyone will be willing or able to share the thinking we've been exploring with you. However, don't worry, you don't need everyone. A few people you can really share things with is all anyone needs. (And more than many people ever find – usually because they never try.)

Chapter 5

When Will You Find The Time ?

In this chapter we hope to help you *manage* your time more efficiently. This means both more time available for your studying and more time for all those other things you want to do.

Time is one of the few things that is given to all of us in an equal daily measure. To hear people talk, it wouldn't appear to be shared equally!

'If only I had more time. . .!' How often have you used these words? How long is the list of wonderful things you'd do if you had more time? But what happens when you *do* get some 'extra' time – say when a meeting is cancelled, or you finish something early? Do you immediately start off on one of those things you'd do if only...?

'Well, I can't work all of the time' you may be thinking – and of course you're right. We all need time to ponder, to reflect – and to do nothing at all. We're not computers, built to be plugged in 24 hours a day, seven days a week.

Let's explore how you feel about finding the time to study. Please try SAQ 5.1.

SAQ 5.1

How do you find time for your studies? Tick one or more of the following. Then turn to our responses to the options you chose.

- I make precise plans – for example Thursday evenings 2000–2130, Saturdays 1015–1230, etc

- I hate plans. I work when the mood takes me

- I just can't work during the week – I've no time. I can however get some longish spells of work fitted in to the average weekend

- I tend to do a bit of studying whenever there's nothing else crying out to be done

continued ↓

- I travel around quite a lot, and use some of this time for studying
- When I've a lot to do, I set the alarm one hour earlier, and put in an hour before the day really starts
- My life is full – I just don't know where I'm going to find any time for studying!
- I've not ticked any of these – I'm different. (If so jot down the ways you can get your studying done.)

But I've still not got enough time!

After reading our responses to the options in SAQ 5.1, you should be realising that different people go about finding time in all sorts of ways. We're all different: there's no reason why we should approach studying in an identical way. We do, however, need to make sure that *enough* (or better, a little more than enough) work gets done. As long as we manage to do this, everything else should take care of itself.

However, maybe you're still feeling that finding time is difficult. If so, try SAQ 5.2, but don't look at the response till you've finished it. (You can, of course, read on further.)

SAQ 5.2 A sample time audit

Take any day – a working day or a weekend day. As exactly as you can, jot down one- or two-word descriptions of what you do in each half-hour time interval in the grid below. You *are* allowed some sleep, some food – and to do all the things that you normally do!

```
0000.................................. 1200......................................
0030.................................. 1230......................................
0100.................................. 1300......................................
0130.................................. 1330......................................
0200.................................. 1400......................................
0230.................................. 1430......................................
0300.................................. 1500......................................
```

0330..	1530..	
0400..	1600..	
0430..	1630..	
0500..	1700..	
0530..	1730..	
0600..	1800..	
0630..	1830..	
0700..	1900..	
0730..	1930..	
0800..	2000..	
0830..	2030..	
0900..	2100..	
0930..	2130..	
1000..	2200..	
1030..	2230..	
1100..	2300..	
1130..	2330..	

How long does it take to do something useful?

'What's a reasonable length for a study spell?' is a question which produces a range of answers. We all have our own ideas of how long is 'reasonable'.

Of course, it all depends on how efficiently the time is being used. It's no use sitting for an hour, turning a page now and then – but with *nothing happening*. Does this ever happen to you?

Let's explore the consequences of 'how long?' responses. Try SAQ 5.3 now.

SAQ 5.3

What do you think is a 'reasonable' approximate length for a typical study spell?

- 3 hours
- 2 hours

continued ↓

- 1 hour
- 30 minutes
- 15 minutes
- something else.

Now please check with our response.

Concentrating and studying

We've already seen that concentrating is something we can only maintain for limited times. Especially when it comes to learning something new. It's as though our brains are only capable of taking in so much in any one spell. This sometimes makes progress seem difficult, especially when you've got your non-studying life to live as well. There is good news however: things get easier the more times you've tackled them.

Let's take two cases.

Case 1

Suppose for the sake of argument you had to learn how to solve a difficult mathematical problem. Suppose you struggled with it – and eventually solved it after 90 minutes. Then you moved on and studied other things. Suppose three months later, you came back to that first problem. It would probably take you quite a long time to remind yourself how to tackle it.

Case 2

Suppose you had the same mathematical problem, and it took 90 minutes to crack it first time as above. Then suppose *next day* you did it again (or did a very similar one). That would take a lot less than 90 minutes, because you can still remember how to go about solving it. Suppose you did the same (or similar) problems every few days for a month. By the end of that time you'd be able to do such problems in a very short time (maybe five minutes!) because you'd hardly ever need to stop and think. You'd almost be able to do such problems on 'automatic pilot' and be certain of getting them right.

There are two morals wrapped up in these cases. Firstly, don't try to use all of your time forging ahead: it's well worth using much of your time practising things you've begun to master. This saves time in the long run.

Secondly, some tasks take longish spells of time (tackling something new for example) while other tasks take much shorter spells of time (going over something you've already cracked, and need to continue to remember).

Keeping to schedule

By now, you'll have gathered that we're not recommending any sort of rigid schedule – the sort that you'd rebel against sooner or later anyway. We're recommending 'targets'. You're well up to target if you can answer 'yes' to one simple question: 'Am I doing enough?' It doesn't matter whether it's all on Sundays, or half-an-hour every day if you can answer 'yes' to that. So a schedule is not so much to do with how long (or at what times) you fit in your studying, but more to do with getting through what you need to in the overall timescale you face (for example getting through a syllabus in good time for an exam).

What if the answer to 'Am I doing enough?' is 'No!' Let's explore some of the things that could make this happen.

SAQ 5.4

Select any – or all – of the following reasons why you may feel 'behind schedule'. Then look at the responses to this SAQ for tips about how to avoid such problems in the future.

- People want me to do other things
- The TV tempts me away from studying
- Doing household jobs and duties
- Boredom or exhaustion
- Distractions from neighbours or family
- My natural tendency to put things off
- I get discouraged by the amount of work.

Towards being a **full-time** *part-time student!*

Full-time students have just as many problems with time management as part-time students – and they've got fewer excuses! It's mostly a matter of attitude towards time.

If studying is felt to conflict with all the other things you want to do – and all the other things you *need* to do – it's little wonder that the time for studying seems perpetually difficult to find. If, instead, you regard your studying as an essential part of your life, time begins to appear from nowhere.

Don't segregate your studies from the rest of your life – *build them in*. Even when you're doing all sorts of other things, no one can stop you *thinking* about your studies every now and then.

Always have something connected with your studies *with you* – at all times, wherever you go (within reason!). If you've got something with you, when a few spare minutes come up, there's something you can do. If you have nothing with you, you can't! A single folded sheet of paper with some key points written on it is enough – or a book, or a card with some questions written on it, or a list of important formulae, or a sketch. The list of possibilities is endless!

Capitalise on spurts!

Most learning happens in spurts! It doesn't happen in slow, controlled transfusions. Even if you're sitting for a solid two-hour spell, the real learning tends to happen in spurts. You can capitalise on spurts. Build more spurts into your lifestyle!

When studying is part of the fabric of your life, your subconscious mind will be beavering away making sense of things you've learned, and seeking information about things you haven't yet mastered. (If you segregate studying to isolated parts of your life, you deprive yourself of most of this subconscious learning.)

But some tasks **need** *longer times!*

This is true – to some extent. Writing an essay may require a longish sitting – at the final stage. Similarly, writing a report takes time. The danger is that you may be tempted to use such things as an excuse for *not* doing things that can be done in spurts. You may say to yourself 'there's no point me doing anything till I've got that essay out of the way.' It sounds plausible, but by now you should realise it's just a putting-off device.

Even some of the longer jobs can in fact be done in spurts. Writing this book was a 'longer job' for both of the authors – but neither of us had any 'longer times' to do it in. So we did it in spurts! We think in fact it turned out better that way. Every time we came back and looked at bits we'd written, we saw new things we needed to write about. This wouldn't have happened if we'd just sat down and tried to write it all at once. Our subconscious minds were working on the things we wanted this book to do, as we went about our normal work and play.

Quality, *not quantity*

In this chapter we've spent some time looking at ways of getting enough time for studying, but so far we've not said much about *quality* of studying. In fact, quality is by far the most important side of things – and we'll really get stuck into that from Chapter 7 onwards. *How* you study is much more important than how long you study – and that's good news for all of us for whom time is precious. By 'quality' we mean studying in a way that has high learning payoffs. After all, what really matters is the quality of your learning – not how long it took you to do it.

Review

We started this chapter dealing with 'If only I had time....' It turns out that time is not the problem it appears to be – it's the way you approach *using* the time available to you that matters. This may be a suitable point for you to write one or two resolutions about your plans to maximise your use of time. If you dare, write them out and stick them up where other people can see them – and help you stick to them!

Chapter 6

Where Will You Study?

In this chapter we hope to help you to:

- abandon your search for a learner's paradise!
- make the most of the various learning environments available to you
- explore what can be done with 'unlikely' learning environments
- blend your studies into the whole of your lifestyle, rather than confining them to a 'tidy corner' of your life.

Where's best for you?

We often ask full-time students this question. After all, not much of their *real* learning happens during class time. All students need to do a lot of work on their own: being a part-time student simply means you'll have to do that much more under your own steam.

When we ask a large group of full-time students where they learn, their answers will be roughly like this: some will say 'in my bedroom', others will say 'in the library', and many will say 'at home, on the dining room table'. Some – usually only a few – will say 'wherever I can'.

As a part-time student you are unlikely to have the sort of purpose-built study-bedroom that some full-time students have (those, that is, who are lucky enough to get into halls of residence). You probably won't be able to get to a library as often or as easily as they can. At least, it could be difficult to carry all your learning materials in and out of your local library any time you choose. So, let's see where you'll be studying – try SAQ 6.1.

SAQ 6.1

How are you fixed for a place to study?

- I'll have to sort out a suitable study area at home

- I've no problem, I've already got a good place for studying at home
- I'll have to go out to study, maybe to a library or some such place
- I'll be doing much of my studying at work, where I have a suitable place
- Help! I really don't know where I'm going to find space to do my learning.

So where is the best place?

Think back to our responses to the options in SAQ 6.1. We made cautionary comments about most kinds of places for studying. There's an even more important danger: imagine you have an excellent place (home, work, wherever) – somewhere that really suits you. You study efficiently there. What's the danger? Try the next SAQ.

SAQ 6.2

What's the main *danger* of having a good place to study?

Our advice is to become able to do a bit of studying almost wherever you are. Make studying a real part of your whole life, not just something that happens in a particular room. You don't have to be studying 'hard' in all of these places. For example, a little gentle revision of material you've already covered can be done almost anywhere – and can be immensely valuable over a period of time.

'But I can only really get down to serious studying when I've got all my materials to hand' is a myth! True, there are some things you do where you need most of your materials – but not many! In fact, you can only read a page at a time – so you only need *one* thing to read to be able to do some reading. You can only write with one pen at a time (unless you're an advanced ambidextrist!) so you only need *one* surface to do some writing. And some of the things involved in studying don't even involve pen or paper – they just need your brain. And you've got that with you everywhere!

We're certainly not advising you to carry around all your learning materials with you all over the place. All you need with you is 'something' related to your studies. Later in this book we'll go into what the 'something' can be. You'll find that there are many possibilities. If the 'something' is small and pocketable, the chances that you'll use it in the odd few minutes that go spare increase. You'll become able to do useful little bits of studying even in the oddest places!

One of the authors of this book learned first-year chemical kinetics in the front seat of the top deck of double-decker buses! He had a 40-minute journey each way every day. He got into the habit of pocketing a snappy little textbook on the subject, and using it on every journey – but only for a few minutes every now and then (when he'd already looked at everyone else's newspaper within eyeshot!). He did manage to use it *actively* though – testing himself mentally on bits of it, then checking to see if he was correct, and so on. He found at the end of the year, when preparing for the chemical kinetics exam, that he had very little learning still to do. It saved him maybe 30 hours of serious revision time! He passed that exam, and chemical kinetics became a favourite topic. He lectured on it later for years!

Working in odd places

Let's imagine there's one vital bit of information you really have to learn well. It may only take five minutes to do it. It's night, and it's raining outside. Imagine you do this (don't do it, just think about it!):

> *Pick up a torch and an umbrella, go outside with the bit you're going to learn, spend five minutes learning it, then come back in.*

Our guess is that you'd remember that bit of learning very efficiently. Simply because you'd done something so different, it would stick in your mind. That might have been an extreme example, but do you see the principle involved?

It's to do with 'association'. If you can 'hook up' the thing you're wanting to remember to something else memorable, it's much easier to recall the thing concerned. We're not suggesting that you do all of your learning in unusual places. But if you have something with you, and a few spare minutes, there's no reason for not doing a bit wherever you are, when the mood takes you. If you didn't have something with you, you wouldn't have the choice of doing a bit. In fact you'd have a reason for not doing anything: an excuse!

The place to study is where you are!

Think of all the places you spend time in during a week. These could include:

- your workplace
- your home
- your car
- on trains
- on buses
- sitting in the park
- up a mountain
- on a boat.

We've already explored (in Chapter 5) how long it takes to get something useful done – and we hope you're convinced that it's minutes, not hours. Think next about some of the things that are involved in your studying:

- writing notes
- preparing written work to hand in
- reading books and journals
- learning key ideas
- deciding what's important
- practising answering questions
- discussing topics with other people
- finding the useful parts of learning materials
- deciding what you *don't* need to learn
- thinking about things you've just learned
- deciding what you need to ask someone
- deciding who to approach to ask questions.

Now think of some of the things you may need to have with you to do tasks such as those above:

- a pen or pencil
- some paper to write on
- something to place things on
- books and journals
- your notes
- your brain!

All that remains is to decide *what* you can do *where*. You can't write notes easily while driving a car, but you can still be *thinking*, and even reciting into a cassette recorder. You can also be listening to *recordings* you've made of key information you wish to remember.

The same applies to most of the places you spend time in during any typical week. There are things you can't possibly do in some of the places, but there are useful things you *can* do almost anywhere.

Let's bring all these ideas together – try SAQ 6.3 now.

SAQ 6.3 'A space audit'

List below half a dozen places you spend time in during a typical week, then alongside jot down some study activities which you could do in each of the places.

Place   Activities possible

-
-
-
-
-
-

Review

How many times have you had a flash of inspiration in the bath or on the golf course or at the dinner table? Could you have gone somewhere special to have such flashes of inspiration? We think not. We hope you're now convinced that your studying should follow you around wherever you are. If studying is part of your whole life, it's likely to be more efficient and more productive. If studying were to be confined to a few hours in a particular room, it wouldn't really become part of your lifestyle.

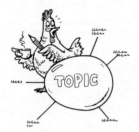

Chapter 7

How Can You Make Studying Really Efficient?

In this book we've already looked at some of the main issues in getting down to studying, including:

- why?
- when?
- where?
- with what resources?

Let's now start to explore *how*.

The word 'efficient' sounds attractive. If you can make your studying really efficient, you overcome many of the problems of limitations on time. You get more done at a time. You keep up to schedule. More important, you have the feeling that you're getting somewhere fast. As a part-time student, time is precious, so anything that helps you get the most from every minute you study is useful.

It's well worth looking critically at various things you do as part of your studies, and finding out which things have the highest payoffs in terms of learning.

Ever had the feeling you're getting nowhere fast as you study? If so, try SAQ 7.1, which explores some of the causes of such feelings.

SAQ 7.1

Tick any of the following that have applied to you (or still apply!).

- It takes me a long time to get started. I sort out all the books and papers I may need. I get a cup of coffee ready. I dig out pens and pencils. I tidy up my desk or table. I tidy up the rest of the room as well. I open the

---

window. I fiddle with the heating level. I do all sorts of things to put off the dreadful moment of starting *thinking*.

- I find it difficult to switch on. It takes me ages to get my mind back into the topic I'm studying. By the time I've really got tuned in, my time is up!

- When I'm writing things (essays, reports, assignments) I find it difficult to be organised. I spend ages before I really get down to putting my writing together.

- When I'm writing, I sometimes go off at tangents. I find it difficult to keep to the point.

- Sometimes as I'm reading, I go into a sort of limbo. I turn the page every now and then, but nothing's really happening in my brain. I dare not look back to what I've just been reading about in case I find that I haven't been taking anything in. So I just plod on, hoping that some of it is taking root.

- When I'm reading, I easily get sidetracked, and read all sorts of things I don't actually need to know. I enjoy this, but it doesn't do my learning schedule any good.

- Although I get to know a lot about things I study, I don't seem to get to know the *right* things! Exams always seem to ask me to do things I hadn't prepared for.

Now please see our response.

Towards efficient studying

Each of the options in SAQ 7.1 represents something that leads to study being inefficient, either by wasting time or by wasting energy in one way or another. Let's follow our exploration of efficiency in the same order as the options in SAQ 7.1. Basically, the danger areas wrapped up in those options are as follows:

- getting started
- telling the difference between work and **WORK**
- switching on and tuning in
- organising written work
- avoiding 'reading limbo'
- avoiding being sidetracked when reading
- getting to know the *right things*.

(The last one of these is SO important we'll save a whole chapter for it – Chapter 10.)

Getting started

Remember all those things people tend to do before really getting started? Why do we do such things? Simple – they're all easier than starting to *think*. It's so easy to potter around, tidying up, getting things together, and thinking about nothing.

The remedy is simple: *start straight away*. You don't need much to start. You can only read one thing at a time – so one will do for starters. Unless you're amazingly accomplished with your fingers and can write different things with each hand simultaneously, you only need one thing to write on. So you don't need a lot of clear space. You don't need *all* the books and papers you may later use – not yet.

Dive in: read something and write something for, say, the first ten minutes. Then start to tidy up, get other books, make some coffee, open the window.... The difference is that you'll still be thinking about the subject matter you covered in those ten minutes or so. This is much more productive than thinking about routine things. A lot of learning occurs subconsciously when we ponder something, reflect on it, gather our thoughts, and so on. You can tidy up and still be learning if you're not just thinking about tidying up. Therefore it's best to take the plunge: start thinking *first*.

Telling the difference between work and **WORK**

Let's think of the work you do in connection with studying as being made up of two (overlapping) categories:

- work: all sorts of things you need to do as part of your studies, but which tend to take a lot of time, and don't amount to a great deal of learning or a significant percentage of your final grade or score. In short: *low* learning payoff.

* **WORK**: really getting to grips with your subjects in a way that guarantees your eventual success; things that have much to do with your final score or grade. In other words: *high* learning payoff.

See what we mean? Let's see if you do: try the next SAQ. Think carefully about this one – it's important!

SAQ 7.2

Here are a dozen things, most of which you'll probably do at one time or another in your studies. Which of these things are which kind of work? Make your choices, then compare with our response.

	work	**WORK**
1 Writing essays		
2 Writing reports		
3 Making summaries		
4 Preparing a seminar		
5 Reading round the subject		
6 Making lists of questions		
7 Rewriting lecture notes		
8 Practising answering questions		
9 Making essay plans		
10 Doing literature searches		
11 Doing set homework		
12 Discussing topics with other students		

Of course, you may well be able to think of other tasks that are part of your studying, and you should now also be able to decide what their relative payoff is in terms of learning.

SAQ 7.3

We've already described two categories of work in terms of high or low learning payoff. There's another difference between the activities that fall into these categories – what do you think it is?

How can you make sure **WORK** gets done?

We've already mentioned how easy it is to put things off. The high-learning-payoff work is probably *very easy* to put off! It's much easier to do something that is fairly routine and straightforward than to do something that involves real thinking and learning.

But you've got a balance to keep. Both kinds of work have to get done amid all the other things in your life. That's why it's worth thinking for a moment about strategy. Try the next SAQ.

SAQ 7.4

Which of the following strategies do you think may be best at helping make sure that a sensible balance is made? And why?

- Every time after doing some work (essays, reports, and so on) do 15 minutes of **WORK**

- Build in study periods deliberately for **WORK** and keep routine work for other times

- Do 15 minutes of **WORK** every time before you settle down to do work of the more routine variety.

Switching on and tuning in

As you'll have gathered from the last section, it's important to start doing something productive (with high learning payoff) right at the start of any study session. We'd like to share with you one way of switching on and diving in. We call it 'laying an egg'. It's a way doing several things, including:

- getting your mind to pick up where you left off from – *quickly*
- preparing your mind to process information about something new
- getting your thoughts organised for putting an essay together, or structuring a report.

You can use the technique in all sorts of ways once you see how productive it is.

Why 'laying an egg'? Because the first step is to draw one! But more importantly, because it is a way of planting ideas firmly in your mind in a way that they can grow, adapt, develop – and 'hatch' into successful deep learning.

Let's go through it in steps with a few comments about each step. By all means try it out for yourself as we go.

1. At about the middle of a blank piece of paper sketch an egg – about normal size. (Takes around one second to do.)
   (Why didn't we say 'draw a circle'? Because people would go and get a compass or a teacup or .... Remember time-wasting strategies?)

2. In the egg, write a word or two. For example:

- the name of the topic you're about to resume studying
- the topic you're about to start studying
- the key words from the title of the essay you're going to put together.

This should only take seconds to do.

3. Look at the topic in your egg, and think of *anything* that relates to it (eg a question, something you already know, something you want to find out, a sub-topic, etc); draw a spoke out from the egg and jot down a word or two about it (ie a question or sub-topic of the topic in your egg).

4. Look back at the egg, and think of another sub-topic or question; draw a spoke and add a word or two.

5. Keep looking back at the egg, and carry on until you've got lots of spokes radiating in all directions – long ones and short ones – each with a word or two at the end. This may take a few minutes. (Don't make it much longer than five minutes though. You can always continue to add to your egg as you study further.)

This technique is one form of 'brainstorming' – allowing your mind to range freely over something, and jotting down a word or two about every thought you get (it doesn't matter at all if some are sensible ones and some aren't – jot them all down anyway). Perhaps we should speak of laying *free range* eggs!

Why keep looking back at the egg? Because it makes sure that you don't wander off on long tangents in your thinking. It helps you keep your thoughts focused on the main idea jotted in the egg.

Why an egg, and not simply a list? The problem with lists is that we write them in a particular order. This tends to set like concrete! It may not be the most sensible order. With a 'spatial' arrangement of spokes radiating in all directions, each spoke looks as important as any other. We can then look at the whole picture while deciding which points are important and which aren't.

6. If you're putting together your thoughts for an essay, or building up the contents of a report, the next step is to look carefully at all the things round your egg, and decide what the most sensible order will be to string them together. You may be looking for one thing leading naturally towards another, or for the order that will have the maximum impact – adapt the technique to the task in hand.

You can then write numbers alongside each of the things at the ends of the spokes and you have a plan for the essay or report. This helps you to get on with the task of writing, without repeating yourself, and without moving awkwardly from one point to the next. It also ensures that valuable ideas don't get forgotten as you get absorbed in the fabric of your writing – your plan remains there to remind you of your original set of ideas. And of course you can always add further ones to the egg at any time and remove any that turn out to be unproductive.

It's time for you to give our method a try – for fun. Try the next SAQ.

SAQ 7.5

'Lay an egg' below with one of the following words:

- tree
- pudding
- river

as though you were going to plan an essay on one of the topics.
Then compare your egg with ours in our response to SAQ 7.5.

'Laying an egg' may seem a far cry from hard work, but in fact it's very close to the **WORK** we thought about earlier.

It's something you can do in a short time, and something that can have a high learning payoff – and that can save you wasting time following up tangents if you're writing something. In exams, most marks are for things directly related to what the questions ask – not for tangents. In exams, tangents cost time. Tangents cost marks.

Organising written work

It's possible to take our lay-an-egg technique further. Once you've made your initial plan for a piece of written work, it's very useful to carry the plan around with you and keep having another look at it every time you get a couple of minutes. You can scribble in little amplifications of each of your main points: just enough to remind you to include things as you think of them.

On separate pieces of paper (or on a wordprocessor), you can draft out the paragraphs that relate to particular points, and gradually collect together the raw material which is going to form your essay or report.

Suppose you've got all the raw material drafted out in this way. What next? Try SAQ 7.6.

SAQ 7.6

Let's think particularly of an essay. A good essay contains three parts:

- a beginning
- a middle
- an end.

In what order do you think it's best to work on these? Jot down the order you think is best, then compare with our response.

Avoiding 'reading limbo'
Have you caught yourself sitting reading for a while, turning the page every now and then – with absolutely nothing happening? Haven't we all! It's not useful work! It's all right if reading for relaxation, but not when you're reading to learn, with time at a premium. How can you avoid 'reading limbo'? Try the next SAQ.

SAQ 7.7

See if you can think of four ways of making sure that the reading you do is productive, and has a high learning payoff. Then compare your ways with our response. If your ways are different from ours you may end up with eight!

-
-
-
-

Avoiding being side-tracked when reading
The trouble with reading is that even when we're reading actively, it's difficult to stop! We tend to carry on reading, even when the text is going way off what we want from it.

It's important to ask yourself one question all the time you're reading:

What could I (reasonably) be expected to become able to do with this?

Every time the answer to that is 'nothing', you're in danger of spending time and energy on something that is not going to have a learning payoff for you. However, whenever the answer to that question is *not* 'nothing', it's best to start doing things to help you become able to do whatever may be necessary. In Chapter 10 we suggest a powerful way of making sure you become able to do the right things.

Meanwhile, one quick way of helping to avoid sidetracks is to create your own agenda before you start to read something. A list of questions you want answers to is a good start. This can be in the form of a 'free range egg' like the ones we described earlier in the chapter.

Summary

We hope that this chapter has given you some ideas which will help guarantee the *quality* of your approach to studying. When time is at a premium, it's not possible to have infinite *quantity* of study – so quality is all the more important. Think of it like this: many full-time students – who have lots more time than you – don't ever really get their act together regarding using time productively. They don't always get high learning payoffs! You can.

Over to you!

Chapter 8

How Can Active Learning Guarantee Successful Study?

The previous chapter looked at ways of making your studying really efficient. This chapter takes that theme further and offers you suggestions for a wider range of activities to help you to learn.

In this chapter we:

- make a distinction between passive learning and active learning
- begin to explore with you what examiners are looking for in good examination answers
- offer you a wide range of activities to help to make your learning more efficient
- reflect on the notion of active learning.

Let's start off actively – try SAQ 8.1.

SAQ 8.1

What have the following activities got in common?

- Listening to a lecture
- Reading a textbook
- Reading notes that you have previously made from lectures and from textbooks.

continued ↓

The problems of passive learning

Our response to SAQ 8.1 referred to passive ways of learning. This can be contrasted with active ways of learning. Listening to lectures, reading textbooks and reading notes that you've previously made from lectures and books can all be done sitting down, moving only your eyes and your ears (moving your *ears*? – you know what we mean!). Your attention span when you're in such a passive mode is likely to be limited to about 20 minutes or less. The more passive you are, the shorter will be your attention span. The way most of us fall asleep is to become as passive as possible! Small wonder that we say you also need to engage in other learning *active-ities*!

Here's yet another thing that all the activities in SAQ 8.1 have in common. They're all about inputting information into your head. Unfortunately, most examiners are not primarily interested in how much information you have in your head or how much you have managed to remember. Examinations that only require students to 'regurgitate' what they have memorised are held in low esteem by college staff. Exams that test only short-term memory are usually regarded as poor exams.

Exams test the results of active learning

Most exams are looking for evidence that you have mastered the concepts that have been introduced in the course. They're also looking for evidence that you can successfully apply them.

This is not the same as providing evidence that you can remember large chunks of your notes. That's why exams:

- include problems that you haven't encountered before
- ask you to relate concepts to unfamiliar situations
- require you to compare and contrast different concepts

and so on.

In other words, in most exams you're expected to work with the material that you've covered on the course. If all you can do is regurgitate your notes then you won't do very well in exams. This is the reason why people with photographic memories don't come top in all the exams. It's the reason why all the universities aren't full of people with photographic memories. It's the reason why people with pretty poor memories can still do well in examinations. And it's the reason why working very late into the night before an exam (or getting up very early to study on the day of the exam) doesn't make a lot of sense: it's very likely indeed that any additional knowledge you manage to cram into your head will be more than offset by a reduction in your ability to apply the knowledge that is already there.

We aren't saying that you don't need to remember anything. What we are saying is that memorising is *not enough*. We're saying that passive ways of learning aren't necessarily the best ways. We're saying that it would be better to develop a portfolio of learning activities (or a learning 'toolkit') which includes a selection of active learning methods.

Active learning methods

You've already encountered some of them in the last chapter:

- making summaries
- making lists of questions
- practising answering questions
- making essay plans.

These are some of the 'unsolicited' activities that we called **WORK**. These are things with a *high learning payoff*. There's another obvious one: identifying key points.

It's not enough, though, to simply mark them with a highlighter pen. This is not really active enough, though it can be a useful first step.

But these were just for starters: there are many more possibilities. Spend some time with SAQ 8.2. It's the longest SAQ in the book. It's worth doing it for real – it should prove a useful investment for you.

SAQ 8.2

Here is a long list of more active learning methods. Tick a few that appeal to you. Be selective.

continued ↓

SAQ 8.2 *continued*

- Make a list of examples to demonstrate that you understand the concepts and technical terms you're learning

- For each concept, write down an application

- Use the egg technique (from Chapter 7) to make 'egg summaries'

- Make up a glossary of concepts, key words and/or technical terms (which can later serve as a useful revision tool)

- After each lecture (or section of your work) ask yourself the questions: 'If there was only one thing from that lecture that I could choose to remember, what would it be?' 'Now, if there were two things, what would the second one be?' 'And if there were three things, what would the third one be?' You can repeat this with groups of lectures: 'If there were only one thing from the whole of the first term that I could choose to remember, what would it be?' You can do the same with chapters of books, and so on. What you're doing in using this technique is prioritising. It's a valuable process; it makes you clarify the key ideas – the ideas with the widest applicability. And because it's essentially a decision-making process, it's automatically active

- Draw diagrams to illustrate concepts

- Draw pictures to illustrate concepts: use lots of colours and don't be embarrassed about your artistic skills or lack of them – it's the thinking that trying to draw brings you that's your real payoff!

- Draw cartoons to illustrate concepts (cartoons tend to be memorable – especially ones you draw yourself – helping the concepts to stay with you)

- Try to identify:
    - the *strangest* concept or idea on the course

SAQ 8.2 *continued*
- the *most useful* concept or idea
- the *most amusing* concept or idea
- the *silliest* concept or idea
- the *strongest* concept or idea
- the *most boring* concept or idea
- the *sexiest* concept or idea

and so on. Let your imagination have free rein – all this helps your concepts and ideas take root

- After you've made a summary of your notes, make a summary of the summary, then make a summary of that

- Make a note of analogies ('this concept is like x because....')

- After you've answered questions from past exam papers, ask your lecturer to mark them

- Use lecture notes to construct a flowchart or outline of the course

- Write key concepts or key ideas on index cards

- Keep a learning log, ie a diary of your personal learning, feelings, conclusions about your learning experiences, and so on

- Use action plans – lists of items which you would like to accomplish. It's best if the things on these lists are:
  - few
  - uncomplicated
  - specific
  - can be accomplished within a reasonable specified time

- Record a summary of your notes on a cassette and play them back when travelling in your car or using a personal stereo (when you're washing up, doing the ironing, jogging, and so on)

continued ↓

SAQ 8.2 *continued*

- Work through your notes to make a list of all the things that aren't clear to you and then cross them off as you gradually come to understand them

- Offer to give a presentation on what you've learned so far from the course

- Go through your notes and try to think of anything that contradicts what you've written

- For every example in your notes, try to think of a counter-example

- Work through your notes to make a list of all the things that you don't understand and then use this list as the basis for asking questions of your tutor, fellow students or anyone else who may be able to answer them for you

- Relate concepts and ideas from your course to your own personal experience

- Use concepts gratuitously when talking to felow students. For example, if you're doing a course on economics you might find plenty of occasions to speak of 'diminished marginal returns'. You could talk of the diminishing marginal returns from time spent in a lecture, diminishing returns from time spent in a session of reading, diminishing returns to time spent in the refectory, and so on

- Try to find ways of connecting apparently unrelated concepts and ideas together.

This is the end of SAQ 8.2 – for the moment! Now please read our response.

Getting your learning toolkit together

In SAQ 8.2, you've just explored a large range of things that can help your learning be active, and we hope you've ticked many of them as ones that could appeal to you.

Of course, it's no use them just appealing to you if you don't *use* them. Some you can use any time in your studies. Some need to wait till you've got enough to work on (but take care that doesn't become your excuse for not trying them out earlier!).

It's time to make some resolutions regarding trying out the ones you selected (and maybe some others too). Please do SAQ 8.3. Again, be conscientious!

SAQ 8.3

Look back through the options of SAQ 8.2, this time adding more ticks as follows:

- three extra ticks for things you'll try straight away – within the next day or two
- two extra ticks for things that you'll build into your regular ways of learning but not quite yet
- one extra tick for things you'll try out, though you're not sure at the moment how useful they'll be.

This means you'll prioritise that long list – and have some plans for where to start putting some of the ideas into practice.

Active learning with friends

Many of the things we listed in SAQ 8.2 can be done on your own, anywhere, anytime. Many of them can also be done with friends on the course – and may be even more productive done that way. For one more time we want you to go back through that long list in SAQ 8.2 – at least through the ones you have ticks beside now. Please do SAQ 8.4.

SAQ 8.4

This time, put a big asterisk beside those things from the list in SAQ 8.2 that you could do with friends on the course.

Let's go on to explore some ways of really taking advantage of working with friends. SAQ 8.5 lists yet more suggestions for doing active learning – this time concentrating on ones you can do with friends. Try it now.

SAQ 8.5

Work through the list below. First, tick the ones that appeal – then prioritise them as you did with the previous list, ending up with four ticks, three ticks and so on.

- Each of you identify the three *main* points from:
  - a lecture
  - a book
  - a chapter or
  - an article

  then see if you agree

- Each of you go through your notes writing down things you don't understand. Then ask each other to explain things. You'll find you learn a lot when it's your turn to explain – as well as learning when things are explained to you. Finally, make a (short) list of anything none of you has been able to explain. Use this later to ask someone who *can* explain (maybe a tutor, or a student from a later stage on the course)

- Each of you make outline answers to particular questions from past exams, then compare them – see what's not in yours that could have been, and vice versa

- Make up quizzes to test each other

- Brainstorm ideas for things to include in answers to questions from past exam papers

- Simply discuss your work. It's impossible to do this without learning something!

Picking the right tool for the job

Some of the activities in our lists are more applicable to some subjects than to others. Some will appeal to you more than others. Think of these lists as a resource, not a prescription. Select the ones that are most useful to you at any particular time, starting with the present. Keep others up your sleeve for the time when they may give you high learning payoffs.

You may well find that you'll use different tools at the start of your course from those you find most useful when revising later.

Summary

We think passive learning has a small – but important – part to play in an effective learning strategy. The reasons for its limited use are:

- with passive learning, attention spans are shorter
- passive learning is mostly about memorising – but memorising is a relatively small part of what is tested in most exams.

At its worst, passive learning is a 'jug and mug' approach to learning. In this passive approach the tutor is the 'jug' (full of knowledge) who 'pours' knowledge into the learner – the 'mug'!

Figure 8.1 The 'jug and mug' approach

Don't be a mug! When you think about it, no one really teaches you anything – you teach yourself with resources which include tutors and friends.

Active learning is at the other end of the spectrum from the jug and mug approach. Active learning is about identifying and using all of the resources available to you to learn. It's about accepting responsibility for learning as much as you can from your tutors, from yourself, from your friends, and from all your other resources.

Chapter 9

How Can You Get The Best From Your Tutors?

As a part-time student you've got less opportunity than full-time students to see tutors. Your time in college is likely to be tightly scheduled with class attendance. If your college sessions are evening ones you have even less opportunity. Apart from the staff running your own particular classes, tutors are less likely to be around during the evening – and you may not be able to get to college very easily during the day. So it's not so easy to call in to a lecturer's office for a cosy chat about part of a subject that's causing you trouble.

We hope that when you've worked through this chapter, you'll:

- be able to make the most of the limited access that you have to your tutors
- have formed more realistic expectations about tutors
- be able to get better feedback from your tutors
- be able to get better results from your tutors
- view your tutors as human resources.

What's in a name?

We've got a problem of terminology in this chapter which we'd like to clear up at the outset. Our problem is what to call the academic staff at the institution of further or higher education where you're doing your course.

On the one hand, most of them probably belong to the National Association of Teachers in Further and Higher Education, or the Association of University Teachers. So it might seem natural simply to call them teachers. Unfortunately, 'teachers' has some inappropriate connotations. Teachers are people that you encountered at school and school was not always a happy experience for many part-time students. You probably don't want your experience of part-time further or higher education to feel like being back at school.

We don't want you to feel like being back at school either. We want you to relate to the college staff in an entirely different way. For us to keep talking about your 'teachers' is likely to reinforce attitudes you had at school that would be counterproductive on your course. It's sometimes said that the difference between schools and institutions of further and higher education is that the former are *teaching* institutions whereas the latter are *learning* instititions. We think that this is a good distinction as it stresses the fact that you're much more responsible for your own learning than you were when you were at school. So we'd rather not use the term 'teacher' to describe the members of the academic staff who you'll meet on your course.

If you asked the academic staff at your college to describe themselves they would probably use the term 'lecturers'. This is almost certainly how their jobs were described in the job advertisements when they were first appointed and the term that appears in their job descriptions. 'Lecturer' has a very different feel to it than 'teacher'. It feels grander and more impersonal than 'teacher'. It conveys the impression of large characterless lecture theatres where you have little contact with the person at the front of the room other than as a receiver of whatever he or she is transmitting. For many, the term 'lecturer' has a rather forbidding ring about it. Also, you may find that most of your contact with a 'lecturer' is not, in fact, in formal lectures. So we're not very happy using the term 'lecturer' either.

It's for these reasons that we've decided to use the term 'tutor' rather than teacher or lecturer.

How do you feel about your tutors?

Sometimes part-time students get the feeling that they're less important to their tutors than are 'normal' full-time students. It's not so easy to get to know some tutors. Some tutors may seem a bit unapproachable. It's all the more important then to work out ways you can overcome these limitations and get the most out of having tutors.

As a part-time student, it's possible that you are rather different from the average full-time student in the way you feel about tutors in general. Try the next SAQ – explore how you feel about tutors.

SAQ 9.1

Tick any of the options below which coincide with your feelings about tutors – different options may, of course, apply to each different tutor.

- I feel a bit threatened – especially when faced with the prospect of handing in work for assessment

- I get a bit impatient when the tutor is explaining to the group things I already know

- I don't like asking questions – I'm afraid I may look silly!

- Sometimes there's a tutor I just don't like – and I find it difficult to 'warm' to his or her subject

- I really look forward to class sessions – there's a great atmosphere and I enjoy them

- So-and-so is a really splendid tutor – I could learn anything from this tutor

- Some of the tutors make me feel a bit like being back at school, and I don't like that.

Now please turn to our responses to the options you ticked.

Getting your questions answered

As we mentioned in our response to the last SAQ, if you don't do something with any questions you have, the danger is that you'll forget what the questions were in the first place.

The first thing to convince yourself of is that it's all right to have questions that you want answered. If you have no questions perhaps the course is too simple for you – or perhaps you're not thinking hard enough.

Many questions won't require help from a tutor: you can sort them out for yourself or with fellow students. But every now and again there's likely to be something where you need expert opinion. That's where your tutor comes in.

What's the best way of going about asking a tutor a question? Perhaps this is more complex than you think! Let's look at it from the tutor's point of view. Suppose you're a tutor. You're a busy person. You're under pressure at work, with all sorts of things waiting to be done: exams to set, work to mark, lectures to prepare, a book you're writing, and a family that needs your time and attention. Try the next SAQ.

SAQ 9.2
You're a busy tutor. Maggie is a part-time student in one of your classes, and she's got questions she needs to ask you.

How would you prefer her to go about it? Choose one or more from the following. Think about the advantages and disadvantages of each approach.

- Ask questions in the middle of one of your sessions

- Come up to you at the end of the session, and ask questions

- Give you a note saying 'When you've got time, could you glance at these questions, and come back to me with some answers?'

- Send you a note along the same lines as above

- Ring you up at work during the day

- Ring you up at home during the weekend

- Ask Mrs Johnston – a colleague of yours who seems less busy – instead of asking you

- Make an appointment with you to come and see you at a time suitable for both of you.

Now please read the comments about each option in our response to SAQ 9.2.

Asking questions in class
We've already seen that asking questions in a group can be a problem, for example, for reasons such as these:

- no one feels like interrupting the tutor

- part-time courses tend to be ones where there's a lot to get through in a limited time – too limited a time for question-and-answer sessions

- people are afraid of asking silly questions

- no one wants to be the one person who is always asking questions (everyone might groan).

That said, there are powerful *advantages* in asking questions during sessions:

- when Maggie asks a question, there will probably be others in the group who didn't know the answer – and who didn't realise that they may *need* to know the answer

- if most students keep asking questions, the tutor is alerted to the fact that there is a gap between the understanding in the class and the level of the sessions. The tutor then has the chance to try to narrow this gap.

Our response to SAQ 9.2 explored the pros and cons of a number of other ways of getting answers to questions. There are some further ways:

- other people in the class may well be able to answer *your* questions. Also, you may be able to answer some of their questions. The more you work together with a few other members of the class the fewer problems you'll have with unanswered questions

- you can, of course, often find the answer to a question by looking it up or doing a bit of digging in your books or the library. This depends on having jotted down the question! (Ever got out your books, then wondered what it was you were looking for?)

Asking about assessment

Something that both you and your tutor are likely to be deeply concerned about, but which often seems to be pushed to the margin of discussion, is the exact nature of assessment. For example, exams.

On many courses, the exams will be set by your tutors themselves. Even if they're not, your tutors will have a good idea of the sort of questions and the expected standards.

Sometimes there seems to be a taboo on discussions which would help you to gain ideas about the sort of things you're heading for. With some tutors, it's almost as if it's 'not playing the game' to talk too much about exams.

'Please will you tell us all about the coming exam?' is not the best way to draw information from tutors! 'Please tell us what questions are going to come up in the exam.' Even worse! Try the next SAQ.

SAQ 9.3

See if you can jot down some questions you could ask your tutors which would get you some useful information about assessment and which would normally be accepted as perfectly reasonable.

-

-

-

-

-

How does the assessor's mind work?

The thing that you really want to know is exactly what scores marks and exactly what loses them. Some enlightened tutors share this sort of information as a normal part of their sessions. In some courses 'peer assessment' may be used. This means that you work out exactly what the assessment criteria are, and you use them yourself on other people's work (and on your own). Many tutors, however, tend to regard assessment criteria as a bit 'private' and they don't like to be cornered into exposing exactly how they would make decisions on what earns marks and what doesn't. Then you've got to go about your research a little more carefully. For example, if you get a piece of work back with a B (or 65%, etc) you could make an appointment to see your tutor to say 'I'd be grateful if you could give me some advice on the sort of thing I would need to have done to make this a B+.'

Giving your tutors extra work!

Suppose you already have access to past exam papers, and you're doing some (early) practice at answering them. Suppose also you've got a tutor who is very approachable. Here are two things you could try.

> 'If I have a go at one or two past questions, please would you check through them for me and help me find out what I would have scored with them if I'd taken that exam?'

Many tutors will respond positively *if asked first*. Marking is the part of the job that tutors tend to dislike most and there are few things worse from a tutor's viewpoint than being given some unexpected marking to do.

> 'If I sketch out one or two answer plans (for example, an essay plan) for some past questions, please would you look at them, and advise me whether I'm heading towards good answers?'

This can go down well with sympathetic tutors, who can then give you advice of the most useful sort – planning advice.

Naturally, if you persuade tutors to do the sorts of 'extra' work mentioned above, don't forget to convey your appreciation! Don't defend your answers too strongly if criticised. Your tutor didn't expect to volunteer for an extra argument!

Setting your tutors exam questions

This is a more subtle way of finding out more about the sort of thing that you'll be able to do. It's best if you gather a small group of fellow students for this task. The aim is to compose a small selection of 'guesses' at exam questions, and try to find out which of those guesses is 'reasonable' in standard. Obviously, you can't go up to your tutor and say 'Which of these questions are in the exam?' if your tutor has set the exam. If, however, it's an external exam, most tutors would be willing to advise you on whether they think that you've come up with likely questions and certainly whether your questions are pitched at the right level.

If your tutor has set the exam, you've got to be more subtle. It's also important that no one is seen as trying to get extra 'private' information, so it's necessary to come to an arrangement where the questions that you've thought of can be discussed 'in class' rather than informally. You could ask the tutor in advance something like this:

> 'If we give you a list of questions we've been preparing for, please would you simply say "yes" or "no" to each regarding whether it is at the right sort of level, and whether it's the sort of question that we should be able to answer? We're not looking for clues about what the actual questions are – simply guidance about the sort of thing to prepare for.'

Attitudes and beliefs about tutors

So far in this chapter we've focused on ways of getting more value from your tutors in specific areas. Now we want to look for an answer to the question 'What can you do to make the best use of your tutors?' at a more general level. (Don't worry, we'll be getting specific again before the end of the chapter.)

In one sense the question contains its own answer. The answer is: view them as a resource. So the question becomes 'What can you do to make best use of your tutors as a resource?'

You may agree with this attitude in principle but when it comes down to practical situations it's easy for some common misconceptions to get in the way. You'll find some of those misconceptions in the next SAQ.

SAQ 9.4[1]
Tick 'true' or 'false' or 'don't know' to each of the following statements:

1 Most college tutors receive training in how to teach

   True............... False............... Don't know...............

2 The main job of college tutors is to teach

   True............... False............... Don't know...............

---

3   College tutors get promotion on the basis of how well they perform as teachers

      True...............   False...............   Don't know...............

4   Nearly all your tutors will give interesting lectures

      True...............   False...............   Don't know...............

5   Your tutors will have done a lot of preparation for your classes

      True...............   False...............   Don't know...............

6   Your tutors will take a personal interest in you

      True...............   False...............   Don't know...............

7   Your tutors will have little interest in you personally and will resent being bothered about your difficulties

      True...............   False...............   Don't know...............

8   College tutors want students to challenge all ideas and give their own viewpoints in class

      True...............   False...............   Don't know...............

9   University and college tutors don't want you to think for yourself, they want you to simply record everything that they say and regurgitate it in examinations

      True...............   False...............   Don't know...............

10   College tutors are friendly people

      True...............   False...............   Don't know...............

11   You can't teach a subject well if you haven't had first-hand experience

      True...............   False...............   Don't know...............

12   College tutors are able to answer all your questions on their subject

      True...............   False...............   Don't know...............

> Now turn to our response to this SAQ and compare your answers with ours. We
> may surprise you.

If you were keeping score you'll have noticed that we couldn't say an unequivocal
'true' to any of the statements in SAQ 9.4. What are the implications of our
responses? There is no doubt that tutors have a major impact on student attitudes
and performance. Much damage can be done when students have expectations that
are out of line with reality.

We think there are two perspectives that will help you to get the most out of
your tutors:

- Think of your tutors as resources that you can use to help you to learn
- Remember that they are human beings with all the limitations and
  opportunities that that implies.

If you take these on board then you will have found the key to help you to make
the most of them.

How to improve your tuition

A small proportion of tutors are great teachers, most are various shades of average
and a small proportion are poor teachers. Now here's the good news: you can
make a significant difference to how your tutors behave. You're unlikely to be
able to turn a poor teacher into a brilliant one but you really can significantly
improve the teaching that you get. Most students underestimate the effect that
they can have on the quality of the teaching they receive.

The key here is to remember that your tutors are human beings. This means that
they respond like human beings. Your performance on the course will be better
if you get support from your tutors. Your tutors' performance will improve if they
get support from you.

How can you help your tutors to do well? The behaviour of tutors is governed
by the amount of attention they get from their students. There was once a
psychology lecturer whose students conspired to smile encouragingly every time
he used a certain common word. They then monitored his use of the word and
found a big increase over the space of several lectures.

Consider the following two scenarios. In the first, a tutor is addressing a class
of students who are clearly being very attentive. In the second, the tutor is
addressing a class who are conveying a lack of interest by talking to each other or

looking out of the window. Which group do you think the tutor is likely to be most enthusiastic about teaching? Which of the groups would *you* be most enthusiastic about teaching? Which group is the tutor likely to be prepared to work hardest for? Which group is likely to get most value out of the tutor?

So one way of getting better value from your tutor is to be very attentive in classes. More generally, you can reward tutors for engaging in behaviour that you like. When your tutor does something that you regard as good teaching let your tutor know that you like it.

SAQ 9.5
Your tutor has just given a better lecture than usual. Tick the option below which you are most likely to do:

- Tell your tutor after the class that you liked the lecture

- Tell your tutor the next time that you see him or her in the corridor that you liked the lecture

- Tell your tutor straight after the class what you liked about the lecture

- Tell your fellow students over coffee that you think it was a better lecture than usual

- Do nothing.

Do you want to know what we think about these reactions? Turn to our response to SAQ 9.5 and find out.

Have you got the message? When your tutor does something that you like, make sure that you let him or her know. Do it quickly and be as specific as you can. Any positive behaviour towards your tutor is likely to engender a positive response.

- When you feel pleased that your tutor has written more comments than usual at the end of the piece of work just returned to you *let your tutor know*

- Participate in seminar discussions as much as you can

- Convey your interest in the subject to your tutor

- If you want your tutors to do something different, let them know. Again, be as specific as you can. For example, if you want your tutor to be clearer in providing instructions for coursework you could ask for written instructions rather than a verbal statement. There is no guarantee that your tutor will do what you ask for but you can be sure that he or she will not if you *don't* ask

- If you have personal, work or domestic problems that interfere with your work on the course, let your tutor know. You'll find that most of them will be understanding. They'll know that the reason for your reduced performance is external to the course – and they'll appreciate your letting them know that.

On the other hand, there are certain things that you can do to reduce the value of your tutors as resources. In general, negative behaviour on your part will tend to stimulate a negative response from your tutor. What can you do to make your tutor feel defensive, angry or unmotivated? How about these:

- Miss classes. When you miss a class you are conveying a message to your tutor that you don't value what they are doing. Most part-time students are going to miss a class occasionally due to work pressures or domestic responsibilities. Most tutors appreciate it if you tell them in advance. This helps tutors feel that they are valued and respected

- Turn up late to classes. There will be times when this is inevitable for most part-time students. Again, letting the tutor know the reason helps them feel valued and respected

- Carry on private conversations in class

- Whisper comments to a neighbour in class on what the tutor is saying

- Try to score points off the tutor or other students

- Conspicuously convey the fact that you're bored

- Bitch to other students about your tutor. This can result in the other students behaving negatively to your tutor – which will result in poorer performance.

We are not suggesting that tutors are an endangered species or a bunch of wimps who can't cope with normal robust behaviour. Walter and Siebert (1987) address the issue thus:

> Instructors (tutors) are human beings who react to pressures, demands, problems, stresses, and all the other factors that complicate our lives.
>
> Instructors are human beings just like you. They prefer to be treated nicely. They want you to come to their classes and learn every good thing you ever wanted to know. Most instructors will work overtime to help you. If you'll look for the good in your instructors and try to make their classes pleasant and enlightening, most of them will do everything humanly possible to make your life as a student a good one.
>
> ... What we're suggesting to you is the simple fact that *you make a difference!* You can choose to help your instructors be better instructors who enjoy teaching or to behave in ways that cause instructors to be unhelpful and boring. (p 159)

To be fair, most part-time students, with their greater maturity, are more aware of this than most full-time students. This is one of the reasons that so many tutors prefer to teach mature part-time students rather than school-leavers.

So the upshot of this discussion is do whatever you can to create a climate in your class in which your tutors can do well.

Review

As a part-time student, much of your work will be done with learning resources of one kind or another: books, notes, libraries and so on. We hope that this chapter has convinced you that your tutors are a powerful learning resource – they're not just teachers. You can choose to get the most from these human resources. When doing so, however, you need to treat them with all the sensitivity needed by fellow human beings – not just like a textbook to be opened now and again and then discarded.

In order to make the most of these human resources you need to hold this question in your mind: 'What can I do to help my tutors do better?'

Note

1   The idea for this SAQ and some of the pages that follow it were drawn
     from a book written for American college students by Tim Walter
     and Al Siebert entitled *Student Success: How to Succeed at
     College and Still Have Time For Your Friends* (4th edition, 1987,
     published by Holt, Rinehart and Winston.)

Chapter 10

How Can You Find Out How Well You're Doing?

'How am I doing?' is a question which is on any student's mind. It's a natural thing to want to find out about. There are several things you can do to find out.

As a part-time student, this question is probably even more important to you than it is to full-time students. They have more opportunity to 'compare notes' and find out how they're doing relative to each other.

Sooner or later, other people (using a method called 'assessment'!) will find out how well you've been doing. But that could be too late! The best thing to do is to find out for yourself *early* and regularly – so that you can ensure that you're ready in good time for other people's scrutiny. In this chapter, we'll explore various ways you can find out how well you're doing. Or find out how much you've still got to do.

Getting to know the right things

It's important to make sure not only that your work is productive, but also that you learn the right things. We'll spend the first part of this chapter looking at a technique which can help you identify exactly what to learn, and give you the chance to check that you've mastered it.

When exams or other formal assessments come along, you'll be answering other people's questions. Other people (as well as yourself) will then discover how you're doing. But you don't have to wait until other people ask you questions – you can start asking yourself questions as soon as you like. The sooner the better.

Why ask yourself questions?

Sooner than you may think, you'll be expected to have done your bit. It's amazing how fast time flies when you're studying part time! It seems no time at all before the exams are upon you.

Then, you'll be expected to be able to:

- *do* things
- *explain* things
- *prove* things
- *decide* things
- *review* things
- *calculate* things
- *list* things
- *describe* things
- *deduce* things
- *discuss* things
- *draw* things
- *compare and contrast* things
- *state* things
- *evaluate* things
- *define* things
- *illustrate* things
- *outline* things
- *show the relationship* between things
- *summarise* things ....

You can add to this list.

Can you imagine any exam paper without several of those 'instruction' words? Words like these are the most important parts of most exam questions.

After you've done a bit of studying, you may feel that you know something quite well. How can you measure whether it's well enough? How can you test for anything that may have slipped? How can you make up for the fact that for most of your time you've not got other students around against whom to compare your progress?

The best way is to *ask yourself* questions, give yourself tasks to do with the knowledge you have. So let's move on to ways of storing questions for you to practice with.

Collecting questions

Suppose you had a small notebook filled with all the questions you could possibly be asked about your course material. Suppose, next, you gradually got yourself into the happy position of being able to answer most of these questions at any time. Exams would be no problem. But how can you decide which questions to collect? By asking yourself one, important question (we mentioned it a little while ago):

What am I (reasonably) expected to become able to do?

Suppose you keep asking yourself that question all the way through your studying – lectures, notes, handouts, textbooks, literature extracts, everything! Suppose next, instead of writing down the answers to that question, you turn the answers into short, sharp mini-questions. You could end up with thousands of mini-questions – a 'question bank', along these lines:

- What's a grommit?
- State Parkinson's Law
- Derive the Henderson Equation
- List five features of parbling
- When does grommifaction occur?
- What's the difference between sproggits and spraggits?
- Who first explained antiquarking?
- Compare and contrast plonking and plunking
- Why does submoggification happen?
- Sketch a wobbulator
- How many kinds of queeter are there?

and so on.

Forget the nonsense words – see what we're getting at?

It doesn't take very long to build up a large collection of short, sharp questions. When you can answer all the little questions, you automatically know enough to answer any bigger ones, which are just combinations of your little questions. If you make a comprehensive question bank, and practise with it, you'll automatically develop your ability to answer any exam question that might come up. Have a go at the next SAQ.

SAQ 10.1

Have a shot at starting a question bank with something you're presently studying (or have previously studied). Take only a page or two of subject material (notes, textbook extracts, etc). Take a blank sheet of paper and see how many short, sharp questions you can jot down in ten minutes. At the end of your ten minutes, count your questions and put numbers beside them.

You don't have to be able to answer all these questions straight away, of course – that's where practice comes in. It's still useful to know what you are aiming to be able to answer, even at a very early stage. In fact, it's very useful to find out the questions you *can't yet* answer.   If you know that something is going to take a bit of time, effort and practice to get under your belt, you're more than halfway there.

The biggest danger, in fact, is 'not knowing what you don't know'. In other words the danger is being unaware of the bits of material that could cause you difficulties. Remember the 'unconscious uncompetence' we mentioned in Chapter 4? Far better to turn it into 'conscious uncompetence': then you can do something to turn it into a competence. With a good question bank, you quickly discover what you *don't* know, as well as the good news about what you *do* know.   You're then in an ideal position to work on the things that you still need to polish up.

The main part of a good question bank is the collection of hundreds of short, sharp questions. However, there are some valuable additions which can make your question bank even more comprehensive and useful. Try SAQ 10.2 now.

SAQ 10.2 Question-bank components

We've suggested using lecture notes, handouts and textbooks as sources of questions for your question bank. Now see if you can list other sources which can help you to extend your question bank. Try to think of various sources of questions that you can use as you go through the day-to-day processes of your course. Think now about 'ready-made' questions, rather than the 'mini' variety.

- lots of mini-questions from lecture notes, handouts and textbooks, etc.

Other sources of questions:

-

-

-

-

-

-

Now compare your ideas with ours – see our response.

'Prompts'

It's also useful to make a 'bank' of clues, cross-relating to your question bank. That's one reason why we suggested numbering your questions – you can number the clues in the same way. (No use having the wrong clue for the wrong question!) By 'clues' we mean something that will help you on your way towards the answer, should you be stuck. Think of them as pointers or hints. A clue should be just enough to get you on the right track towards the answers – but still leave you with some active thinking to do on the way.

Clues are better than answers. As soon as you see an *answer* you rob yourself of the chance to think it through. When you see a clue, you still have to make that extra little leap towards the answer. The more often you make such little leaps, the more you'll remember making them.

SAQ 10.3

Take that sheet you made when you did SAQ 10.1, and on the reverse jot down a clue (not an answer) for each of the short questions you wrote. Then put the sheet somewhere where tomorrow you can have a further go at answering the questions – this time with the help of your clues for any questions where they're needed.

With practice, you'll be able to sit in an exam room, and think back to your clues and leaps, and come up with the answers you need to exam questions.

The question bank (and clues) is an example of what we call 'learning tools'. It's something that, once made, can be used again and again. There's a high learning payoff in the act of making it in the first place – and a high learning payoff every time you use it. (Like all tools, however, it will go rusty if you don't keep it in use.)

Armed with a good question bank, you're able to know the answer to that question that is always at the back of your mind: 'Am I doing sufficient work?' You can measure your progress at any time, not just when preparing for exams. You can measure your progress from day to day, well before any formal assessment is due.

Making the most of tutor feedback

We've already explored how useful it is to engage in continual self-assessment. That's where your question bank comes in. However, every now and then, you've the chance of assessment from tutors. This is likely to help you find details of the sort of standard that is being looked for in exams.

How useful this is depends a lot on how you react to feedback from tutors. Let's see how you react at present. Try the following SAQ.

SAQ 10.4

Suppose you've handed in a piece of work for tutor assessment. For the sake of argument, let's say you've just got it back. It got a grade D (or a score of 45 per cent), and your tutor has written various things all over it. How would *you* react?

- Bin it!

- Feel bad about the score, and too angry to read the feedback comments

- Feel bad about the score, and quite argumentative about the feedback comments

- Forget the score, and look carefully for what you could glean from the feedback comments.

As you should now be realising, scores and grades are just one kind of feedback. The comments are usually much more important.

We looked at the case of a low score. The danger of ignoring feedback comments is just as great with a high score. If you get something back with an A+ on it, it's (pleasantly) tempting not to bother with what your tutor said about it. But you could be ignoring very useful information.

Making the most of other people

Write down one word to describe the following: 'Other people's opinions of what you are doing wrong.'

What word would you use to describe this? Think of one before going on to the next paragraph....

Was your word a negative one or a positive one? Some people would call this 'criticism'. Some people would call it 'feedback'. What's the difference between criticism and feedback?

Getting feedback – 'oops-a-daisy!'

Getting feedback is very important to learning. It's an important way of finding out how you're doing. It's even more important than that: it's also an important way of achieving goals.

Stewart Emery, in his book *Actualisations,* illustrates this by reference to the inertial guidance system used by aircraft. The inertial guidance system of an intercontinental aircraft is designated to get it to within 1000 yards of the desired runway within five minutes of the estimated time of arrival. It does this despite the fact that the aircraft is off course for 90 per cent of its journey!

The way it works is like this. Every time the plane strays sufficiently off course, the pilot makes a correction. Emery reports a pilot as saying: 'So the path from here to where we want to be starts with an error, which we correct, which becomes the next error, which we correct and that becomes the next error which we correct. So the only time we are truly on course is that moment in the zig-zag when we actually cross the true path.'

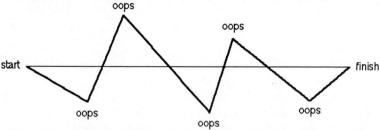

In other words, the inertial guidance system uses feedback to correct errors to stay on course. You can think of this as the 'oops-a-daisy' system.

This system means you have to make sure that you get the information that would tell you when you're going off course. This may imply a fundamentally different attitude from the one you usually adopt. You may not enjoy hearing that you're off course. Our message here is that rather than minimising the amount of criticism/feedback you receive, try to maximise it! Your route to your destination will be more direct if you get feedback as soon as you start to go off course. This means that you'll waste less time and energy heading in the wrong directions.

The benefits of looking for feedback

Are you the sort of person who is reluctant to do anything unless you're sure you're right? Can you see how this might limit the amount of feedback that you receive? The trick is to worry less about making mistakes, and concentrate on correcting mistakes that you make.

This perspective has a number of implications. First, you can't know what corrections to make if you don't know where you want to get to.

If you don't know where you want to get to you're likely to wind up somewhere else.

After working through the first chapter of this book we hope you have a pretty clear idea of where you want to get to through your course.

Secondly, the more that you can increase the flow of feedback to yourself the more you can stay on course. This is another reason for developing your support network. The most important people in your support network for providing feedback are likely to be some other members of your course. If you find a few people on your course whom you can get along with, you can increase your potential for success. If you find a few others on the course with whom you can feel comfortable and trusting, you can increase your potential for success even more. If you can work as a *team* to share ideas, feelings of high and low morale, thoughts on course content, books, notes and so on, then you'll greatly increase your potential for success.

Thirdly, a valuable attitude to have when you make a mistake is:

There is no failure, only feedback.

The amount of feedback that you get is likely to reflect your attitude to receiving feedback. People are reluctant to provide feedback to those who receive it as criticism, or to those who interpret it as failure, or to those who react to it defensively.

You may have heard the story of the king who slew the bringer of bad news. Not very fair and not very sensible! He found considerable difficulty recruiting reliable messengers! If you give a hard time to those who give you feedback when you're going off course, guess what you'll get a lot less of? You've got it – feedback. If you don't get much feedback from others it may be because they see you as someone who can't handle it.

SAQ 10.5

What would you be most likely to do about a friend on your course who has bad breath? And what would you be least likely to do?

continued ↓

- Tell your friend directly
- Send your friend an anonymous note
- Nothing.

Before turning to our response to this SAQ, reach a clear decision about which you would be most likely to do and which you would be least likely to do.

Fishing for feedback
So what can you do to increase the flow of feedback that you get? Here are some ideas.

- Ask for it (encourage others to give you feedback)

- Ask the providers of feedback to be more specific

- Don't be defensive – you don't have to explain or justify or retaliate

- When the feedback is positive, accept it – don't shrug it off

- Thank the providers for it

- Trade it ('I'll proof-read your essay if you'll proof-read mine').

Getting feedback is really important to achieving your goals and your education. When your goal is successfully to complete a course of education it becomes doubly important.

We keep stressing the importance of other people in your success on your course. Now we're going to link this with those question banks that we talked about earlier in this chapter. We've already explored how you can use them to quiz yourself. We've already seen how useful they can be for finding out about the bits that slip.

By now you'll have guessed how useful it can be to get other people to quiz you. This adds reality to the game. The 'other people' could be fellow students, but they could also be friends, relatives, partners – almost anyone. Even if the person who quizzes you with your question bank doesn't know the answers to the questions – and doesn't know what the questions mean – you still gain the experience of being put on the spot. Anyone can tell when you're bluffing an answer. Above all, *you* know.

You may have to do a bit of persuasion to get some people to help you, but if you let them know how valuable their help can be to you they're not likely to refuse. Of course, you must let them see how much you appreciate their help. There are plenty of ways you can show this.

Another advantage of getting other people to ask you questions is that they can rearrange the order of the questions and the wording – and even the content. The more you develop your ability to cope with the unexpected, the less you'll be thrown when the unexpected turns up.

The ideal situation is where you've got some fellow-students who are also committed to the idea of question banks. You can take turns in quizzing each other. You can find out more about how you are doing by comparing with how they are doing. A busy little study syndicate can be a very productive way of working. No doubt about the high learning payoff that is possible with this sort of work. People in a good study syndicate realise that there's far more mileage in cooperating with each other than in competing. Remember, it's the standard expected of you on the course that matters.

Avoiding the slide!

The title of this chapter was 'How can you find out how well you're doing?' It was *not* 'How can you tell how well you did once!'

The point we're making is that when you've mastered something, it's no use just hoping it will stay mastered. Think back to that competence model we explored in Chapter 4. What happens to any competence if it isn't regularly polished?

Take driving for example. If you drive, when you passed the test you were probably consciously competent at driving. After a while, you probably became even more competent, but less conscious about it. If you look about you on the roads, you'll see many people who are unconsciously *uncompetent* as drivers! The same sort of thing can happen to anything you learn to do. The simple solution is to test yourself at regular intervals.

There is no need to make a fetish of this. You'll often be pleasantly surprised at how much has stuck. You'll also be surprised at how easy it is to 'recover' things that you once knew but which have become a little rusty.

Only if you are in the habit of checking occasionally that you still can do the things you've mastered will the answer to that question, 'How am I doing?' be 'Just fine!'

Chapter 11

How Will You Cope With Revision And Exams?

As a part-time student, you're short on two things which help full-time students prepare for exams:

- time
- constant company of fellow students.

This does not mean you've no chance! Many full-time students waste a lot of their revision time, and never find out how to put to good use the company of fellow students. Studying part time simply means that it will pay you to make sure that your preparation for exams is *efficient, effective and economic*. Economy – of both time and effort – is far more sensible than stretching yourself beyond reasonable limits. After all, if you're going to succeed in your exams, you have to survive revision!

We've divided this chapter into three sections:

- Section 1: Mainstream revision
- Section 2: Just before your exam
- Section 3: Playing the exam game.

However, before we get into an exploration of revision and exams, let's look ahead to what exams measure. See if you can guess. Have a go at the next SAQ.

SAQ 11.1

You're judged a lot on the basis of your exam results. What are these results actually measuring? Select one or more of the ten options below, then check our response to each option to see whether your thinking converges with ours.

My exam results are a measure of:

1	how much I know
2	the quantity of revision I've done
3	how intelligent I am
4	the quality of revision I've done
5	how much practice I've had at answering exam questions
6	how well I can spot exam questions
7	how quickly I can write in exams
8	how good I am at managing my time in exams
9	how good I am at addressing the question in exams
10	how much I managed to learn the night before!

Now that we've looked ahead to the day of reckoning – exam results – let's start thinking about how to guarantee that they will do you credit. As we mentioned, we'll use the rest of this chapter to help you explore revision and exams – in three stages: mainstream revision, just before your exam, and playing the exam game.

Section 1: Mainstream revision

What's revision?
Silly question? We all know what revision is. But do we? If we were all skilled at revision, everyone would pass exams with flying colours. So what goes wrong?
When you've studied this section, you'll be better able to:

- fight the urge to put revision off

- make more efficient use of your revision time

- turn your revision into practice at passing exams

- build your confidence and morale by keeping track of what you can do, rather than what you can't do!

Let's explore revision, starting at the beginning. How early should you start? Try the next SAQ.

SAQ 11.2

When do *you* start revision? Choose from the following options the one you think fits you best:

- I manage to put if off for ages, until it's really rather too late

- I start gently quite early, then build up to high efforts as the exam gets nearer

- I forget things easily, so I deliberately leave revision till near the exam

- I don't do any special 'revision', I work steadily all the time and don't need an extra boost near the exam.

Now please look at our responses to the option you picked – and the others.

So what is *revision?*

Back to that question again. It's not so much the quantity of revision that matters, it's the *quality* that brings you success. As a part-time student, you haven't got all the time in the world to do vast amounts of revision, so its all the more important to make sure that you make your revision as productive and efficient as you can. For a start, there isn't just one thing called revision, there are lots of different activities that you can choose from. Try the next SAQ now and see if you recognise quality when you see it.

SAQ 11.3

Below is a list of various activities that may come under the heading 'revision'. Look at each in turn, and decide whether it is high, medium or low quality. Look again at each activity, this time deciding whether it needs to be done alone, or could be done better with fellow students.

1   Reading and rereading all your notes and books
2   Digging in the library to find as many extra sources of information as you can

3   Writing out your notes again and again
4   Looking through old exam papers and trying to spot likely questions
5   Practising answering questions, sometimes mentally, sometimes in note form, sometimes in full, sometimes against the clock
6   Working through your materials, devising your own questions, and practising answering them
7   Working with fellow students, quizzing each other on likely questions
8   Getting someone who doesn't know anything about your subject to quiz you on it (giving them a list of questions to ask you of course!)
9   Building a glossary for your subject material
10 Prioritising key points for each section of a topic
11 Making a list of concepts, and for each concept identifying as many uses as you can.

Were you surprised how many kinds of activity we listed? Revision isn't just one thing! Now please check our responses to each of these options, and see if you agree with the points we make about each of these kinds of revision.

After reading our responses to the last SAQ, you should be thinking that a *variety* of things makes up a sensible revision strategy. But revision is more a state of mind than a particular set of actions. If you get on to that practice wavelength, you'll find yourself doing all sorts of things which involve practice – mental, written, spoken, the lot.

Let's sum up so far:

- Start revision early. It doesn't matter if you forget what you learn! It'll be easier and easier to relearn it
- Focus revision on practice at what you're preparing for – *answering questions*
- Where possible make good use of fellow students. This makes revision more sociable – and much more productive.

The final few weeks: the hard slog?
Can you remember that hard slog just before exams? Did you enjoy it? Or did you enjoy when it stopped? All sorts of things go wrong during hard slogs. Look at the list below, and tick those which apply to you.

- I can be sitting, turning the page every now and then, with *nothing happening*! If someone asked me what I learned half an hour ago, I wouldn't have the foggiest

- I am very good at finding things which have to be done before I get back to my books – shoes to clean, washing-up to do, a trip to Tesco's, the kids to see to, a bill to pay, a letter to write.... (Please add a few of your own!)

- I sit staring at the telly for ages, trying to pluck up the energy to get back to my studies. I don't actually enjoy what I'm watching

- It's so much nicer chatting to friends or family than sitting working alone. I seem to have a lot more to chat about during 'hard slog' times

- I get into a state of panic and depression. I feel that I'm forgetting things faster than I'm learning them

- The sheer boredom of sitting with my books for hours on end gets to me. I rebel: 'Why did I start this?', 'Does it really matter?' and similar questions erode my better intentions

- 'I'm only a *part-time* student after all'; all the other things in my life simply make this sort of hard slog impracticable.

How many of those did you tick? Well done if you ticked none of them. You've probably sorted out a strategy to cope with the dangers lurking behind each of them.

If you ticked some (or all) of them – even better. Let's explore what you can do about it. We'll explore each of them in turn, and see what the remedies are.

I can be sitting, turning the page every now and then, with *nothing happening*! If someone asked me what I learned half-an-hour ago, I wouldn't have the foggiest.

The problem here is simple, if common: your mind is rebelling against the boredom of sitting for long spells with your study materials. The brain switches off when it gets bored. The remedy is common sense:

- Work for short spells – lots of them
- Change topics frequently – a change is as good as a rest
- Make your revision more active – practise answering questions. This is far less boring than just reading.

I am very good at finding things which have to be done before I get back to my books – shoes to clean, washing-up to do, a trip to Tesco's, the kids to see to, a bill to pay, a letter to write. . . . (You may have added a few of your own.)

Most people are expert at putting off revision. The simple truth is that all these things are *easier* than getting down to serious work. Some people will redecorate the whole house in an attempt to avoid the evil moment of doing some real revision! Here's a good remedy: do a short spell of revision *before* you clean your shoes, *before* you go to Tesco's, *before* you pay that bill, *before* you write that letter, and so on. That can add up to a lot of short spells of productive work. A lot of short spells add up to more than one long (boring) one.

I sit staring at the telly for ages, trying to pluck up the energy to get back to my studies. I don't actually enjoy what I'm watching.

Again there's a simple cure: use the telly as a reward instead of an escape. Fit in half an hour of revision *before* that favourite programme. Or use a video recorder to save your favourite programmes till you've earned them.

It's so much nicer chatting to friends or family than sitting working alone. I seem to have a lot more to chat about during 'hard slog' times.

Most people are sociable animals. It goes against human nature to sit for long periods in solemn isolation. Some of your revision may need to be done by yourself, but there's plenty you can do with other people around. Get them to ask you questions – preferably ones you know the answers to. It's still good practice.

I get into a state of panic and depression. I feel that I'm forgetting things faster than I'm learning them.

That's a common symptom of the hard slog. It's mainly due to two things: tiredness, and finding out the hard way how many things you still *don't* know. It's usually the result of having left things too late, and not choosing the most sensible ways of revising. It is preventable:

- Start early
- Build revision on *practice*, so you always know what's still to be done, rather than finding out suddenly at the end that there's a lot to do

- Work with other people, so that any feelings of panic or depression can be talked about – this usually makes it feel a lot better. (Don't, however, work with manic depressives or colleagues of a hysterical disposition!)

The sheer boredom of sitting with my books for hours on end gets to me. I rebel. 'Why did I start this?', 'Does it really matter?' and similar questions erode my better intentions.

Two main factors cause this problem: 'hours on end' and lack of variety.

- *Don't* sit for hours on end. A lot of short spells adds up to something much more valuable than one boring long spell

- Keep the variety going:
  - a bit of reading
  - a bit of thinking
  - a little written practice
  - a little verbal practice
  - another go at something that went wrong once
  - list some key points
  - make some entries in your glossary
  - brainstorm the uses of a concept
  - prioritise the importance of some facts
  - a little of two or three different topics rather than a heavy chunk of one topic.

I'm only a *part-time* student after all; all the other things in my life simply make this sort of hard slog impracticable.

All the suggestions to the problems we've looked at so far involve management of effort, to ensure that your revision is efficient and effective. As a part-time student, you need to be good at managing your time too. Several things can help with time management during the later stages of revision.

- Don't wait for a two-hour period where you can get down to it. Use the easier-to-find quarter-hours at various parts of your day

- Don't leave all your revision to the ends of your day, or to weekends. Do a bit (just a little is enough) *before* going to work, *before* breakfast, and so on. This activates your subconscious mind

- Always have something *with you* – at work, in the car, on the train. Just a little is enough. In fact, the smaller the chunk of material you have with you, the more likely you are to find a few minutes to work with it. Make cards summarising the main points you need to remember. These can be used anywhere, at almost any time. Make cards with exam questions on them, and scribble down outline answers.

We've now explored all seven of those things that may go wrong during revision. Do you now feel more confident that you can avoid any of the things that may have gone wrong for you? The way to failure is paved with good intentions – so make sure that your intentions are turned into *actions*.

By now, you should be feeling that the old-fashioned 'hard slog' is quite redundant. Effective, efficient, economic revision is not at all like that sort of hard slog. High-quality revision is less boring, more active, more social, less time-consuming and more *enjoyable* than that hard slog.

Let's end this section with a reminder of ten foundations for high-quality revision. This time, beside each of the suggestions, write your own action plan – a few notes to yourself about how you're going to turn your intentions into reality.

Action plan

1. Start revision early
   For me, this means...

2. Avoid long spells of just reading
   For me, this means...

continued ↓

---

3.   Practise answering questions
        For me, this means...

4.   Get other people to ask you questions
        For me, this means...

5.   Work in many short spells rather than a few long ones
        For me, this means...

6.   Make use of odd bits of time – before breakfast, lunchtimes, on trains...
        For me, this means...

7.   Give yourself variety – don't plod on with one topic for too long
     For me, this means...

8.   Practise important things many times, making sure you can apply what
     you've learned to new situations
     For me, this means...

9.   Keep checking to find out what you may have forgotten – it's very
     useful to know what's likely to 'slip' – so you can stop it slipping
     For me, this means...

10.   Deal with all those plausible reasons (excuses!) for not doing a little
     revision!
     For me, this means...

The more notes you made above the better. Once you've decided what's sensible, it's not to hard to *be* sensible!

Section 2: *Just before your exam*

When you've explored this short section, you should be less likely to:

- give yourself a hard time in the last few hours before any exam
- arrive at your exam desk hot and bothered.

How do you feel at the start of an exam?

It's perfectly natural to feel a little excited as the moment of truth approaches. It's all right to have a little extra adrenalin in your system. This can actually help you give good answers. But it's not good to arrive at your exam desk so tense that you can't relax enough to work out what the questions mean. It's not good to arrive so tired that you haven't the energy left to put your answers down clearly on the paper. So in this section we'll explore a few suggestions to make sure that you arrive in a fit state to do yourself credit. These suggestions are no more than common sense, but for many people there's a tendency for common sense to go out of the window where exams are concerned. If you already do everything we suggest, simply congratulate yourself.

The day before – or sooner

- Check carefully that you know exactly when your exam is. You'd be surprised at the number of times a candidate turns up exactly one hour late – and even one *day* late. Such things are entirely avoidable

- Make sure you know exactly where your exam is. Imagine how damaging to your morale it is to find out at the last minute that you're in the wrong building

- Check out the exam room before the day of the exam, so it's not totally unfamiliar to you when you take the exam

- Put together all the things you'll need during your exam – pens, drawing instruments, calculator (with new battery, just in case) and so on. This saves scrabbling around at the last minute searching for that favourite pen.

To work or not to work?

Suppose your exam starts at 0930. Suppose you get up at 0430, and read all of your material between then and the start of the exam. You may well know a lot, but you could be too tired to do yourself justice with the questions! The same goes for working late into the night before the exam. You're marked on what you do *during* the exam, not on the work you did in the 24 hours before.

Most exams test not only whether you know your subjects, but also whether you can use the material you know. When you get tired and overstressed, your ability to use what you know falls off rapidly.

It takes some doing to resist working just before an exam. If you feel you *must* be doing something, make it gentle revision. Keep to things you know rather well already – there's nothing worse than finding out there are things you don't know at the last minute.

If you really want to worry, try worrying hard for half an hour without stopping! Few people can! It's a useful way to get the worrying out of your system – you'll soon get fed up with forcing yourself to worry hard!

The day of reckoning

Your objective should be to get to the exam room without wasting energy, and in a calm, relaxed state. There are some simple things you can do to help ensure this.

Set out in enough time. Be prepared for any eventuality – the car not starting or the bus not coming or the train being late. Imagine how damaging to your morale it would be if you had some such emergency, and spent time wondering if you'd make it in time!

When you get there, avoid the pre-exam ritual. Do you know it? That group waiting near the exam room, where the conversations you'll hear go something like this:

'Do you think there'll be a question on lompicality?'
'Have you read Chapter 5 of Sanderson?'
'I can't understand the principle of compacity at all!'
'I'm not looking forward to this exam at all.'
'Can you draw a cross-section of a grommit?'
'I'm depending on a good question on quobbles.'

Every time you hear something that you don't know, you get more demoralised. You hardly notice when people talk about things you *do* know.

One way out of this is to find a coffee machine about five minutes' walk from the exam room, and not used by your colleagues!

Don't worry! Keep calm...and so on! It's easy to say these things. 'How can I keep calm?' you mutter. It's perfectly natural for you not to feel particularly calm. You are entitled to feel a bit stressed. Allow yourself your feelings, don't try to smother them. It's amazing how when you permit your feelings to surface, they subside quite a lot all by themselves. Remember what we said about worrying hard for half an hour? Even in the exam, you can afford some time worrying hard if you really enjoy doing this – but it's far nicer to do something constructive instead. There are things you can do to relax a bit, such as taking a stroll, a few deep breaths, a chat to someone not involved with your exam. And don't worry about being worried! A little extra adrenalin in your system can actually help you rise to the occasion.

Section 3: Playing the exam game

The rule of the game is simple: within the time allowed, score as many as possible of the available marks.

Why is it that so many students seem to use the following rules?

- Don't read the question properly
- Spend half the total time on the first question you answer
- Write down all you can about the first word you see that you know something about
- Whenever possible, go off on tangents
- Never look back to make sure you're still answering the question as asked
- Spend twice as much time on question-parts carrying five marks as on those carrying 15 marks
- When in doubt, make it up
- Avoid using your judgement
- Don't come to any conclusions in an essay
- Avoid showing how you got to your answer in a calculation.

The rest of this section is going to help you to use the first few minutes of the exam wisely and productively, address each question consistently and with good focus, use the final part of the time allowed to score quite a few extra marks, pass – and do yourself justice!

The first few minutes
In some ways this is the hardest time. It's always a bit exciting when you are confronted with the questions you've been leading up to for months.

There is some temptation to get stuck in straight away, and write something down as quickly as possible. This may not be the most sensible thing to do, however. There are several things that could be more important. See if you know what these are – try SAQ 11.4 now.

SAQ 11.4
See if you can list five things that you should do before starting to answer any question – and before even *reading* the questions. Then compare your ideas with ours in the response.

Before even reading any of the questions:

-

-

-

-

-

We're still in the first ten minutes, about to read the questions. Well done if the things you wrote before reading the questions included planning out your time. This is very important. Let's take an example. Suppose you have to answer five questions in three hours. The exam starts at 0930. This would be a sensible plan:

0930 Do 'first-ten-minutes things'
0940 Start 1st question
1010 Start 2nd question
1040 Start 3rd question
1110 Start 4th question
1140 Start final question
1210 Do 'closing-minutes' things.
   (more about this later in the chapter)
1230 Exam over – go to pub/coffee bar.

Suppose each of the five questions carries 20 marks. Suppose for sake of argument that the passmark is 50 per cent.

- If you attempt all five questions, you need to score on average ten marks for each to pass. This should be quite easy to do

- If your time-management was at fault and you only attempted four questions, you'd have to score on average $12.5/20 = 60$ per cent – this is rather harder. And if one of the four questions was completely off target, you'd have to score about 17 marks for each of the other three to pass – that's much harder. ($17/20 = 85$ per cent!)

- If you only attempted three questions, just to pass you'd have to average 85 per cent ($=17/20$) on each of them.

It's worth that minute or two planning how long you can give to each question. The real danger is that you get carried away with your first two questions. They'll probably be the ones you know most about. What happens if the time arrives when you should start question 2, but you need 15 more minutes to finish question 1? The sensible thing to do is leave a space, then come back to question 1 later. Questions 4 and 5 may not take as long as the earlier ones, so you may have some time spare from them. And you've still got that extra time you allowed at the end of the exam if all else fails. If you spend too long on any question, you're not likely to be gaining many marks in the 'extra' time – especially on essay questions. The figure shows how marks are earned in a typical essay answer as time goes on.

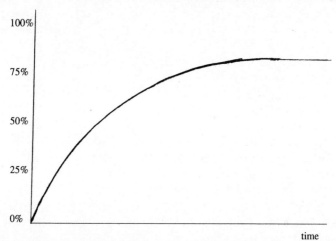

Figure 11.1 *Marks gained over time*

As you can see, it's the law of diminishing returns that applies! You get most marks during the first few minutes, and eventually very few extra marks as time goes on. In practice, the curve does not level out at full marks – examiners always seem reluctant to award full marks, even for excellent essay answers. (With problem-type questions, there's every chance of getting full marks if you get it 'right'.)

The logic is so simple: equal time for equal mark-scoring opportunity. Yet so many candidates seem oblivious to this.

Well, we're still in the first ten minutes – about two minutes into it in fact – and just about to start reading the questions. Let's explore this seemingly straightforward activity in some detail. Let's start with what you think, then compare ideas – try SAQ 11.5.

SAQ 11.5

How should you read the questions? See if you can jot down some things that relate to the way you can get most benefit out of reading the questions.

continued ↓

```
   •


   •



   •




   •





   •
```

From our response you'll have seen that there's a lot more than 'reading' to reading the questions.

So now (at last!) we're at the end of those first ten minutes. Of course, it may be sensible to take even longer over that decision-making part if you need to. Time spent now may save a lot of wasted effort later – such as finding half-way through a question that it's not a good one for you.

Yet more planning?
After you've made your decisions about which questions to do, you may wish to dive straight into your first question, and stick to the timetable you planned. However, there's another way of approaching it: you may wish to spend a few minutes planning each of your answers before you start writing. For example, you may wish to use our 'lay an egg' technique from Chapter 7 with each of your questions, jotting down all the main ideas that occur to you. This can take some of the pressure off your memory. When you first looked at each question, all sorts of ideas would have raced through your mind, and you may fear that some of these would be lost again. Spending a little time planning each answer is a good way of

getting these ideas jotted down quickly on paper, so you don't have to worry about them escaping your memory.

Of course, if you decide to spend this extra time at the beginning on planning, you'll need to make appropriate adjustments to your timetable – you still need to devote equal time to equal mark-scoring-opportunity. Your modified timetable may look something like this:

0930 Do 'first-ten-minutes things'
0940 Spend about five minutes planning each answer
1005 Start writing 1st answer
1030 Start writing 2nd answer
1055 Start writing 3rd answer
1120 Start writing 4th answer
1145 Start writing final answer
1210 Do 'closing-minutes' things
   (more about this later in the chapter)
1230 Exam over – go to pub/coffee bar.

Answering questions and scoring your marks

It's all just a matter of logical common sense from now on. Remember the rule we started with: 'within the time allowed, score as many as possible of the available marks.' Perhaps we should add two more to this:

'all of the marks are available for answers to the question as asked – not for things that the question doesn't ask for.'

'The examiner can only give you marks for what you put on the paper – not for things you know that aren't evident from your answers.'

The main thing is to address each question. Keep rereading the question every few minutes to check that you are still on course and not going off at a tangent. If you're doing an essay question, you could develop the habit of rereading the question at the end of each paragraph you write. (However eloquent tangents are, they simply annoy examiners!)

With essay-type questions, it's well worth spending a few minutes jotting down a plan of the arguments and ingredients you're going to use. (You may well have decided it's best to do this in the 'extra planning' time we mentioned above.) Then think about the way you'll lead in, and the conclusions you'll lead towards – jot these down. Then you can start writing the essay itself, producing it coherently and logically, so that it starts in an interesting way, goes where it promises to go, then comes to a convincing conclusion.

Here are a few tips for getting as many marks as you can squeeze out of the examiner.

- Keep to schedule, within reason

- Keep checking that you're addressing the question. For example, if it asks 'decide' then decide!

- If your questions involve illustrations, graphs, diagrams and so on, make them big and self-explanatory. Make sure everything is properly labelled

- If your answers include calculations, make it easy for the examiner to see exactly what you did all the way along. (If, for example, you made a mistake in the early stages of a calculation, you could end up with zero marks if the examiner couldn't see where you slipped up, or nearly full marks if he or she could see your mistake and also that every other step was correct)

- Make it easy for the examiner to see where each question, and question-part, starts and finishes

- Keep sentences reasonably short. There's more risk of ambiguity with long sentences. Besides, if the examiner has to read each of your sentences three times before he or she can work out what you mean, the 'generosity index' will go down!

Avoiding 'mental blanks'

Ever had your memory go blank on you? Frightening when it happens. Actually, it doesn't just happen, you *made* it happen. What you were probably doing was this: struggling to remember something that you knew was there somewhere, but was lost for the moment. Now, the more we try to force our brains to do something, the more they rebel, even to the point of closing down temporarily!

So if you feel those panic symptoms even just starting, slow down, take a deep breath, and relax. If you were trying to remember something, and it's gone, move on to another question for a while. (It's worth temporarily leaving aside your timetable on such occasions.) Given the chance, the 'missing' bit of information will come back, not long after you've taken the pressure off.

The closing minutes
During the last 20 minutes or so, even if you've still not finished some of the questions, it's worth stopping writing and moving into the following mode:

> **Quickly read through all that you've done.**

You probably won't feel like reading it all, but it's well worth forcing yourself. As you read you'll make several discoveries

- Mistakes. Quickly amend them as you go. Often you will find that what you have written down was not exactly what you meant to say. A few words here and there added in now can rectify that

- Ways of 'tidying up' your script: underlining answers, main points, headings, ruling off between questions or sections

- Bits you missed out, things that have come back into your mind since you wrote your answers: quickly slip them in.

If you use these closing minutes like this, it is possible that you could gain more marks in this time than in the preceding hour! It's amazing how many candidates write down things that they would immediately have realised were wrong if they'd ever looked at the answers again. The examiner may even be able to tell that what was meant was different from what was written, but can't give marks for such guesswork, only for what's there.

After your exam
If you only have one exam, you can do whatever you like after it – you'll know how to celebrate! What we're thinking about is when you may have a group of exams. If you do the 'wrong' things after the first exam, say, it can demoralise you so much that you fail the second one, and so on.

SAQ 11.6

What are the 'wrong' things to do after an exam? See if you can think of what to avoid, and why. Then compare your thoughts with ours in the response.

What to avoid:

Why to avoid it:

Review

In this chapter, we've been exploring ways of making sure your revision is productive and efficient, and that your performance in exams does you justice. We've been looking at the skills connected with doing well in systems where exams count a lot. These skills are just as important as having a good grip of your subject material. Your exam results are just as much a measure of your revision skills and exam technique as your ability in your chosen discipline. What's more, the skills we've been exploring are transferable skills. Once you develop them, you can apply them to all future occasions in your career where you need to master new topics, and demonstrate your mastery, whether in written form or by being able to answer people's questions confidently and effectively.

You may well have revised and taken exams many times in the past. You may have done so successfully so far. But there is always the risk that your old techniques are not quite up to what's needed for your next exam, and there's no time like the present for taking stock of your skills – and taking on board any new ones which may help you get better results. Good grades give personal satisfaction of course, but they also help give you added confidence and can improve your career prospects. The more choice you open up for your future career, the better your chances of finding real job satisfaction.

The word 'satisfaction' says it all. If, when you get your exam results, your revision and exam skills are proved to be all you need them to be, then you'll feel highly satisfied.

Chapter 12

Staying The Course
('I've started so I'll finish.')

This chapter is different from the other chapters. For one thing there are no SAQs. But this doesn't mean that we won't be asking you to do some things which we think will help you.

There's another difference about this final chapter. Most of this book has been about how to succeed on your part-time course. In this final chapter we'd like to start by looking at the other side of the coin. A majority of those part-time students who fail do so before they ever reach the examinations. They do so when they drop out of the course at some stage before the examinations. Of course, for many of them 'failure' is the wrong word to use for this. For example, leaving a course because you discover that it isn't going to meet your needs could be regarded as a success rather than a failure. However, for many of those who start a part-time course but do not complete it, it *feels* like failure.

So what can you do to reduce the likelihood of failing to complete your course? In our research for this book we discovered higher-than-average drop-out rates for:

- those who regarded the information that they obtained before starting the course as 'poor' or 'very poor'
- those who reported the difficulties overall as greater than expected when they enrolled
- those who had missed more than 5 per cent of their classes
- those who had changed their employer whilst on the course.

The first two of these factors emphasises the importance of finding out as much as you can before enrolling. The third factor argues for not missing classes if you can possibly help it. And the last factor is an illustration of how disruptive to part-time study significant personal changes can be. If you are anticipating a period of major changes in your circumstances (changing job, changing house, changing partner!) it would be wise to ask yourself if this is the best time to undertake a course of part-time study. Would you be best postponing it for a year?

Our researches also identified groups with lower-than-average drop-out rates. They include:

- those who had studied at the same college before
- those who first heard about their course from someone currently (or previously) enrolled on the course
- those with friends or partner already taking the course
- those who rated their fellow students as being 'very supportive'
- those who rated the college staff as being 'very supportive'
- those who rated their 'spouse/partner' as being 'very supportive'.

The first three of these factors again stress the importance of getting as much information about the course beforehand as possible. Clearly, those who had studied at the same college before and those who knew someone with first-hand experience of the course or college are likely to have been better informed as a result.

The last three of these factors emphasise the fact that your most powerful resources are human ones – your fellow students, your tutors and your family. Cultivate and develop these resources – they're the keys to your success on the course.

One other human resource is the most important key of all. Yourself. We've covered a lot of ground in this book about how to cultivate and develop yourself as a resource to help you succeed. We hope, for example, that when you discovered in Chapters 3 and 4 what competences you already have at your disposal it boosted your confidence and helped to give you the right attitude to win. We weren't kidding when we chose the words 'How to win' in our title. We now want to look more closely at winning attitudes.

Attitudes

In Chapter 10 we asked you to write down one word to describe: 'Other people's opinions of what you are doing wrong.'

We saw that from one perspective this word is criticism and from another perspective it's feedback. It depends upon your attitude.

Trish is a woman who spends most of her time alone doing things by herself. What one word would you use to describe her?

Please don't read on until you you've thought of a word.

Some people would see this Trish as 'lonely'. Some people would see her as 'self-reliant'. It all depends on your attitude.

How about this one – find one word for 'An obstacle in the way of getting what you want or accomplishing what you want to achieve.'

Did you come up with a positive word or a negative word for this? How about 'problem' (negative)? How about 'challenge' (positive)? Once again, it all depends on your attitude. As a part-time student you're likely to encounter plenty of difficulties. We believe that after working through this book you're well prepared to handle the difficulties – but the difficulties will still be there! And much will then depend upon your attitude to them. The most helpful account of 'difficulties' that we've come across is by Tony Larson in a book entitled *Trust Yourself:*[1]

Do you know what a challenge is? It's a difficulty that you want to solve. It's what you need to make life an interesting, fun game.

Do you know what a problem is? It's the same thing as a challenge – it's a difficulty – only we often don't want to solve it so we don't let it be part of our game.

Amazing isn't it? People want challenges. They don't want problems. But the only difference between those things they want and the ones they don't want is that they look at challenges with a positive attitude and problems with a negative one. Challenges and problems are the same thing – you're what distinguishes them from each other because you're the one who decides whether you want to enjoy solving them or hate solving them.

Let me say it again: there are two kinds of difficulties in this world: problems and challenges. A problem is a difficulty that usually comes in the form: 'Oh no, what am I going to do? Gee, I don't know, what am I going to do? Boy, I don't know; there's not much that I can do. Yeah, I know, so what am I going to do?' In other words, a problem is a difficulty which – to anyone else at least – gets boring after a while. 'Uh-oh. Here comes Edith with her "problem".'

A challenge, on the other hand, is a difficulty that is fun, exciting. We live for challenges. We actively seek out difficulties that are challenging because we enjoy trying to solve them. The first people to climb Mount Everest knew it would be difficult, but that was the excitement of it. Imagine what it would be like to change the challenge of mountain climbing into a problem. 'Hey, men, we've got this mountain to climb.' 'Oh no, how are we going to do that? 'Gee, I don't know; no one's ever done it before.' 'Oh, that's just great. Then what are we going to do?' 'Boy, I don't know, there's not much we can do.' 'Yeah, I know, so what are we going to do?'

Notice how quickly the difficulty got boring when it moved fom 'challenge' to 'problem'? As you can see, the same difficulty can be a problem for one person and a challenge for another. That's because problems and challenges don't exist 'out there' – they're in your head.

We all want difficulties in our lives – that is, we all want things that are hard to do, that take effort and planning, and maybe are even gruelling. We all want difficulties so that life isn't boring. Why do people have children? Why do people knock themselves out to play sports? They don't have to play tennis or swim or water-ski. They knock themselves out doing these things because they want to. People who climb mountains don't do it because they have to – people *choose* difficult things to do....

Now, you may be saying to yourself, 'Change my problems into challenges? How can I do that? Gee, I don't know, how can I do that?' You see, you're already making the transformation of problem-to-challenge a problem instead of making the transformation of problem-to-challenge a challenge....

A large part of changing a problem difficulty into a challenging difficulty is to simply change your way of looking at the difficulty. The power is within you – of course! It's how you choose to look at life and deal with it. You can either go around complaining that rosebuds have thorns – or else you can rejoice that some thornbushes have roses! They're the same thing. You're the one with the power to see them differently. (pp 226–8)

So you want to successfully complete a part-time course of study? Well remember those words: 'We all want difficulties in our lives – that is, we all want things that are hard to do, that take effort and planning, and maybe are even gruelling.' Most part-time courses involve some hardship, take effort and planning and can, at times, be a bit gruelling. Even though you've got the power within you to see difficulties as challenges rather than problems it won't always seem that way. And that's why we offer you the following ideas which we hope you'll find helpful.

It's easier to see difficulties as challenges when your morale is high. When your morale is high you're optimistic, confident, cheerful and disciplined. You feel that you can cope with difficulties that would otherwise floor you. Clearly, it would be helpful if you could sustain a high morale while on the course. Failing that, it would be helpful if you could at least predict when your morale will be high and when it will be at a low ebb. Forewarned is forearmed – you'd then be in a better position to plan appropriately.

Let's take these in reverse order and consider first your level of enthusiasm about the course. You may be enthusiatic now about your course but will it last? Is it possible to predict the level of your morale over the course? Strangely enough, even though we don't know you, we believe that we can. This is based on our experience of other part-time students.[2] We believe that for most part-time students morale varies over the academic year in the following way: it increases at first as students get to know each other and are reassured that they can cope with the course; it then falls, bottoming out around the middle of the year before recovering. The middle bit is known as the mid-course blues. Tutors get them too! They're catching.

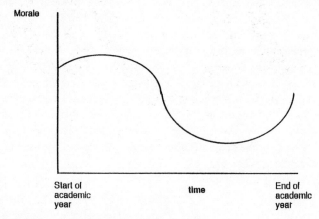

Figure 12.1 *Morale level over an academic year*

So you can expect that your morale and enthusiasm, along with that of your fellow students, will decline around the middle of the year. And you can draw reassurance from the fact that it *will* climb back up afterwards. We hope that the knowledge that it will recover will sustain you when the going gets tough.

So now you're forewarned about the way that you're likely to feel about the course over time. Now for the bigger problem – oops – challenge. Can we offer you any ideas to sustain your morale and reduce the depth of the mid-year downer? One idea that we suggest is to ensure that you maintain a balanced range of activities in your life. Now this really is a challenge for part-time students as your course will be absorbing time that you would otherwise be devoting to other activities in life. We believe, however, that there are some powerful reasons for ensuring that there is balance in the directions that you channel your energies into.

First, consider what happens when you focus your whole life on one area.[3] Suppose, for example, that your're a workaholic and you job is your whole life. This is what life seems like if work is your whole life:

Figure 12.2 *Job is whole life*

Now suppose that you lose your job. Then life would become like this:

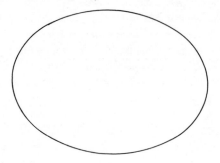

Figure 12.3 *Whole life without job*

Small wonder that many executives whose jobs and careers have been the centres of their lives have great difficulty coping with unemployment. It's not surprising that they feel empty and are desperate to find a new career to fill the emptiness. Small wonder that some people who have lived their entire adult lives focused almost entirely on their job and careers fall apart when they retire. Small wonder that some women who have focused almost all their attention on their children feel empty and depressed when the children leave home. Small wonder that many part-time students feel a sense of loss when they've completed their studies. (But there's an easy cure for this one: there's no need to stop learning!)

Another consequence of what happens when you focus your entire life on one area is that your mood becomes very dependent upon what is happening in that area. So our workaholic becomes very elated when getting praise from the boss and very down when an initiative at work fails. Life becomes an emotional roller-coaster ride. Now suppose that our workaholic enrols on a part-time course to enhance his or her career. What happens when a 'downer' at work coincides with the mid-year blues on the course? Probably quits the course.

Alternatively, you can make sure that you maintain a balanced range of activities in your life. What would constitute a balanced range of activities? We suggest that you begin to answer this question by considering the areas of your life that are of key importance to you.

Imagine a spoked wheel. The wheel is balanced when all the spokes are about the same length. When they're not, you're in for a bumpy ride.

In Figure 12.4, we've labelled each of the spokes with a dimension of your life.

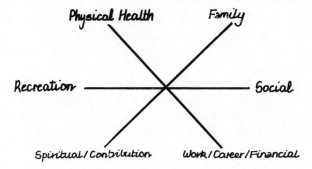

Figure 12.4 *The wheel of life*

We want to help you to find out how 'balanced' your life is. In Figure 12.5 each of the spokes has been marked from 1 to 10. Now we'd like you to consider how satisfied you are with your current state of progress along each of these dimensions (0 = disastrous, 10 = total satisfaction). Please be clear that we are not asking you to rate yourself against others, we are asking you to indicate how satisfied you are with your progress along each of these dimensions – this is a very subjective assessment. So, for example, if you consider the spiritual dimension of life to be unimportant then you might be very satisfied that the spiritual dimension plays little role in your life. Others may feel that this is the most important dimension and may be far less satisfied even though they devote much more time to it. If you're disabled you may rate yourself highly on physical health if you feel satisfied with the way that you cope with your disability. Remember, you're not comparing yourself with anyone else.

Now we'd like you to mark your 'score' on each of the spokes.

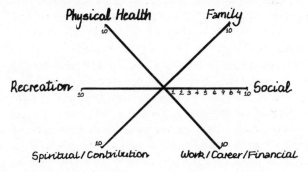

Figure 12.5 *Balancing the wheel*

Finally, we'd like you to join up the marks that you made on each of the spokes. You can think of the resulting shape as your 'life-wheel'. It represents how balanced your life is. Is your wheel pretty symmetrical or is it lopsided? Is one area too close to the centre?

We believe that if your wheel is unbalanced then you'll feel unbalanced and that will be bad for your morale. This exercise will indicate where you need to apply some of your energies to maintain your morale and sustain feelings of wholeness and psychological wellbeing. If you don't respond in this way, then the area(s) that you neglect will be a source of continuing dissatisfaction – they'll clamour for your attention and sap your energies.

There's a bit of a paradox in all this. Here you are taking on a part-time course which will absorb time that you would otherwise be devoting to other areas of your life. And here we are suggesting that you give extra attention to these other areas of your life. There are several ways of resolving this paradox. First, when you lead a more balanced life you'll find that you've got more energy than you had before: you'll be less stressed as you'll have to cope with fewer crises arising from the neglect of important areas in your life. Second, giving more attention does not necessarily mean devoting more time – you can give some of that extra energy to your family in terms of shorter periods of high-quality time rather than longer periods of low-quality time. You can give them time when they have your full attention rather than time when your attention is on work problems or when you are too tired to do anything but flake out. And if you're really creative you can find ways of integrating the various areas of your life. Jog with friends? Go swimming with the family? Ask members of your family to test you on parts of your course that you want to practice?

We recommend that you repeat the 'balanced wheel' exercise every few months (perhaps at the beginning of every term) to help you discover areas of your life which need attention.

And finally ...

We'd like you to think back to things you've learned earlier in your life. The teaching may have taken place in classrooms, lecture halls, laboratories, training centres. But where did the real learning take place? Our guess is that most real learning gets done outside the formal situations such as classrooms and so on. Most real learning is done under your own steam. It's when you get stuck into working with your books and notes or get your hands on the practical equipment, that the real learning starts. In this book we've offered you many ideas about how to make real learning more efficient, enjoyable and more successful.

We're all born expert learners – think about how much you learned about the world in the first three years of your life. Your ability to learn is your birthright. It's only later that we start building limitations to our learning – unnecessary ones!

Learning is a lifelong activity. The real hallmark of success in life – any kind of success – is the ability to learn. Think of anyone whose achievements you admire. They developed their learning skills to achieve greatness. No one but yourself can develop your potential to learn, but others can share with you ideas about learning that you can choose to experiment with. We hope that we've alerted you to the powerful resources within you and around you. Over to you now to put them to work for you.

Drop us a line when you've won as a part-time student.

Notes

1 Larson, T (1979) *Trust Yourself*, San Luis Obispo, California, Impact Publishers.

2 We'd like to thank Behjat Hurren, a student on a part-time degree in business studies at Brighton, who suggested this 'morale index' to us.

3 This idea came from Susan Jeffers (1987) *Feel the Fear and Do it Anyway*, London, Century Hutchinson Ltd.

Feedback To Tom And Phil

We've explored with you the value of feedback – we'd very much appreciate some from *you*. Please jot down your replies to the questions below, then tear out or photocopy these pages and send them to us c/o The Education Editor, Kogan Page Ltd, 120 Pentonville Road, London, N1 9JN, UK.

1   What did you think of the tone and style of this book? Underline words or add your own.

chatty   *boring*   *friendly*   *interesting*   *formal*

patronising *readable*   *stimulating* *dull*   *lively*

2   How useful did you find the SAQs and responses?

very useful *mostly useful* *sometimes useful* *not useful*

3   What did you personally find the most useful idea(s) in the book?

4   What were the least useful ideas in this book?

5   If you could only take two chapters from this book, which two would
     you select – and why?

6   When we write our next book, what would you advise us to do, under
     each of the following headings:

     Stop...

     Start...

     Continue...

7   *What did we miss?* Please tell us any idea(s) of your own regarding being
     successful as a part-time student. We'll mention you in the next edition if
     you give us your name as well.

8   Please add any other suggestions or comments you'd like to give us, or
     details about how your part-time studies are now going.

Thanks for your help – we really do value your comments.

Responses to SAQs, Introduction

Response A

It doesn't matter what you put down for the first part of the question; let's look at the ways you became good at whatever-it-was. Most people say things like this:

- by doing it
- by practising
- by trial and error
- by getting it wrong at first, and finding out why.

The point we make here is that learning is essentially a 'doing' thing. We don't learn a great deal when we read things, unless at the same time we're *doing* something with what we read, such as making summaries, making lists of questions to ask ourselves, and so on. Nor do we learn much just by sitting listening to teachers or lecturers. We've got to start *using* the material ourselves to really start learning it.

(Now that you've seen our response to SAQ A, please return to the text again.)

•••

Response B

Again, it doesn't matter what you feel good about – the interesting thing is how you *know*. Most people's answers to this question involve words like these:

- other people tell me
- compliments from other people
- other people's reactions
- seeing the results of what I do
- other people find me approachable.

In short, the common factors are *other people* and seeing the results. In effect, to feel positive about anything, we all need *feedback*. We need to find out how we're doing. It's all very well to learn things by doing them, but we need to know how well (or equally, how badly!) we're doing them.

Have you noticed something? That's what the 'Responses to the SAQs' in this book are all about: we're giving you feedback. We're letting you know what we think of your answers to our SAQs. The SAQs themselves give you the chance to learn by doing – and our responses give you the chance to get feedback on your own ideas.

(Now, please rejoin the text again. Are you getting used to how this book is going to work?)

• •

Response C

Most people's answers to this question contain one or more of the following:

- I didn't want to learn it in the first place!
- it was boring and uninteresting
- the teacher was awful!
- I was made to feel a fool!
- I just could not make sense of it.

What such replies tell us is that there are two more important conditions for successful learning:

- we need to *want* to learn in the first place;
- we need the time and opportunity to *make sense* of what we learn.

Also, good teaching helps – but let's not worry too much about this. Many, many successful students have learned effectively despite bad teachers!

(Now, please rejoin the text again.)

• •

Responses To SAQs, Chapter 1

Response 1.1

1 **I'm bored and I need a challenge.** An interesting reason. Studying is
   certainly a way of finding challenges and if you were bored you're likely to
   have enough time for study. However, suppose that something else came
   along that seemed more interesting. Would that mean that when you were
   no longer bored you'd give up your studies?

2 **The topic I'm studying will be useful in my job.** That's a good reason for
   studying. It gives you a sense of purpose which will be helpful at those
   times when the studying gets a bit hard. Also, when you can apply the
   things that you study, you get more satisfaction than when you just study
   something in theory with no chance of putting it into practice.

3 **Mastering the topic could lead to promotion.** That certainly can be a
   powerful incentive. However, you might like to think about these two
   possibilities: first, if after studying you didn't get promotion, how would
   you feel? Cheated? Let down? A feeling of having wasted your time? Or
   would it have been worthwhile anyway? Second, suppose that you get
   promoted halfway through your studies. Would you then stop studying
   because you no longer needed to? Thus there are dangers associated with
   this reason for studying, particularly if it is your only reason for studying.

4 **Mastering the topic could lead to more choice in potential employment.**
   That is a very good reason for studying. Psychologists tell us that we should
   change our career direction every few years. This stops us getting stale and
   getting in a rut. It makes life more interesting and challenging. We're not
   saying that it makes life easier – it's often easier to continue what you've
   been doing. However, the more choices you have in what to do, the greater
   the chance that you can choose something that you really like. If you have
   more choices available, your chance of selecting a well paid job is bound to
   increase and so too is your opportunity to make a choice that gives you real
   job satisfaction.

1.1 *continued*

5 **Someone told me to study**. Maybe your employer. Does this mean that
you're only doing it to please someone else or that you're only doing it
because you have to? Does this in turn mean that you resent having to?
None of us likes to be told what we've got to do. The danger here is that
every little obstacle you come across will seem like a mountain. You may
not feel like giving your best when things get a bit tough. If this is your
only reason it may be worth trying to find some extra reasons of your own.

6 **I've always wanted to study this topic and now's my chance.** That's a fine
reason. Many people make this reason work for them. But what would
happen if, when you get a little deeper into the subject, you find it a lot
harder than you expected? Many things are easy at first but get tougher as
you get in deeper. You could sail along while the going is easy and then get
fed up with the topic when it gets a bit harder. So it would be good if you
could build some extra reasons to help you to keep going.

7 **I simply like learning new things.** It's a good reason for studying, as long as
you are willing to keep going when the going is tough. Any worthwhile
programme of study is bound to be tough at times.

8 **A friend or colleague studied it and recommended it.** This can be very
useful because it means that you know someone who has already found the
course interesting and worthwhile. Not all courses can claim to be that! It
also means that you have someone that you can discuss the course with and
find out what it's really like. The course brochure is more likely to tell you
what the course organisers would like it to be. Check out with yourself,
though, that you're not just doing it to prove that you are as good as your
friend or colleague. It might be worth asking what your friend's reasons
were for doing the course and checking whether these are reasons that apply
to you too.

9 **I want to prove to myself or others that I'm up to it.** Be careful here
because proving to yourself and proving to others are separate reasons.
Proving to someone else that you're better than he or she thinks could prove
to be a hollow victory. It would be better if you had reasons that worked for
yourself rather than for other people. Wanting to prove yourself to yourself
is a strong reason for doing it.

1.1 *continued*

Testing yourself in this way can be an important part of the process of self-discovery. But don't be too hard on yourself – it's also important to enjoy your studies. That way success will be all the more certain.

Wanting to prove to the world that you can do it is a reason that has sustained a lot of people throughout a course of part-time study. This means that you want to prove to yourself and others that you're up to it. You know that success will be very good for your self-esteem and your morale.

10 **I want to be able to keep up with and help my children.** Well done! A worthwhile reason for you to do some studying of your own. Besides, when children see parents studying they form the impression that studying is a normal and natural part of life.

11 **To get a qualification for a higher-level course.** That's a good tangible reason for studying. But what if you lose interest in pursuing the higher-level course? Would you then give up? Perhaps you would find it useful to explore your reasons for doing that higher-level course.

12 **To acquire more self-confidence.** This can be a good reason for studying as it is grounded in fact. There is no doubt that for many people a lack of education contributes to a lack of self-confidence. This takes us back to proving to the world (including yourself) that you are capable of successfully completing the course. On the other hand, don't expect a course of part-time study to turn you from a timid mouse into a sophisticated smoothie. Even if you were to desire this, be aware that there are limits to what additional education can do by way of increasing self-confidence.

13 **To broaden my horizons and develop my mind.** It's a good reason for studying, as long as you are willing to keep going when the going is tough. Any worthwhile programme of study is bound to be tough at times. Do you recognise these words? They're the same ones that we used above in response to option 7 ('I like learning new things').

14 **To make up for missed educational opportunities in the past.** This is another fine reason. Many people did not have the opportunity to develop themselves educationally as much as they would have liked. Maybe they had to leave school because of financial pressures at home, maybe their school did not offer the subjects that they wish to study and so on. Some people had the opportunity but did not take it. Maybe they did not realise the importance of education when they were younger, maybe they are late developers and so on. When tutors are developing part-time courses of education they often have in mind those who missed the educational boat first time around.

15 **I've got my own reasons.** That's good. The main thing for you to check out is that they are reasons that will keep you going through rough and smooth. And only you can check that!

● ●

Response 1.2

Before you look at the results from our questionnaire survey remember that they come from students already enrolled on part-time degree courses. Your situation may be very different. If so, bear that in mind when you look at the results. Also, remember that there are no right or wrong answers here. Our aim is simply to assist you in analysing your own aims and sometimes it helps to do this by making comparisons.

Table R1.1 *Main aim when enrolling*

	% of respondents
Improve career prospects	39
Demonstrate ability to complete course	13
Promotion/increased salary in present work	9
Learn more about subject	9
Increase job-changing opportunities	8
Develop mind	5
Improve present job performance	4
Widen horizons	4

Table R1.1 *Main aim when enrolling (continued)*

	%
Compensate for lack of previous educ. opportunities	3
Qualification for higher-level course	3
Acquire self-confidence	1
Relief from usual surroundings/responsibilities	1
Benefit children's education	0*
Make new friends with similar interests	0*
Shared interest with spouse/friend	0*
Total	100**

---

*	Less than 0.5 per cent of respondents.
**	Percentages sum to only 99 per cent because of rounding.

Improvement of career prospects was selected as the main aim by three times the number of respondents that selected any other one of the aims listed above.

The question also asked respondents to indicate the importance of each factor separately. The aims were grouped into work-related aims, subject-related aims, personal-development aims and more general aims.

We got the following results:

Table R1.2 *Importance attached to aims on enrolling*

	Very important %	Fairly important %	Not important %
Work-related aims			
To improve my career prospects:	76	19	6
To improve my chance of promotion/ increased salary in my present type of work:	61	24	16
To increase the opportunities for changing my job:	60	27	13
To help me do my present job better:	38	37	25
Subject-related aims			
To learn more about a subject that interests me:	55	39	7

Table R1.2 *Importance attached to
aims on enrolling (continued)*

	Very important %	Fairly important %	Not important %
To get an educational qualification for a higher-level course:	41	26	33
To develop a shared interest with my spouse/partner, friend etc:	4	17	79
Personal-development aims			
To prove to myself (or others) that I could complete a degree course:	51	29	22
To widen my horizons:	46	41	13
To develop my mind:	42	43	14
To acquire more self-confidence:	23	36	41
General aims			
To make up for lack of educational opportunities in the past:	32	28	40
To benefit my children's education:	13	32	55
To get away from my usual surroundings and responsibilities at home:	9	19	73
To make new friends with similar interests:	6	28	66

Owing to rounding, not all horizontal percentages sum to precisely 100.

Each of the work-related aims was clearly important to a large proportion of the part-time undergraduates. Improvement of career prospects (either in terms of current employment or as a basis for employment mobility) was of key importance. Only 6 per cent of the students rated 'To improve my career prospects' as not important. It seems that part-time degree courses, even in non-vocational subjects, are valued as a means of enhancing economic life chances.

Interest in acquiring a qualification for career advancement is different, of course, from subject interest per se. For 7 per cent of the respondents interest in the subject was rated as not important, 39 per cent reported it as fairly important and the remaining 55 per cent reported that it was very important. The other subject-related aim that was rated as very important by a substantial proportion of the respondents (41 per cent) was 'To get an educational qualification for a higher-level course'.

A substantial proportion of the respondents rated all of the personal-development aims as important. Of this group of aims, the most important was to demonstrate the ability to complete a degree course. This was rated as very important by half of the students and it was the second most frequently cited main aim. Of the remaining aims (those contained in the 'general' category) only 'Compensation for lack of previous educational opportunities' was reported to be 'very important' by a substantial proportion of the respondents.

Responses To SAQs, Chapter 2

There's only one SAQ in this chapter, but it's an important one. We've responded in depth. Please don't read our discussion below until you've done the question yourself.

Response 2.1

Look at the list of potential difficulties again. Which did you tick? Which did you rate as a level-1 difficulty, a level-2 difficulty and a level-3 difficulty?

The purpose of this SAQ was to help you think about the possible difficulties that you might encounter. If you ticked the items that you feel are likely to apply to you and then wrote 1, 2 or 3 against each of the ticks then you've already done some excellent preparation. Well done!

Sometimes, of course, things turn out rather different to what we expect. Enrolling on a part-time course is no exception. In the previous chapter we mentioned our investigation into the experience of students doing part-time degree courses. Some of the findings are also relevant here. One of our questions used the items listed in SAQ 2.1 and asked:

'Have the difficulties of taking the course been greater or less than you expected when you decided to enrol?'

Here are our results (listed in a different order – for reasons we'll explain shortly):

Table R2.1 *Difficulties compared to expectation at enrolment*

	More difficult than expected %	Roughly as expected %	Less difficult than expected %
Finding the time to study:	54	43	3
Coping with competing demands of hobbies or other interests:	43	47	10

Table R2.1 *Difficulties compared to
expectation at enrolment (continued)*

	%	%	%
Organising my time in an efficient way:	39	54	7
Coping with job demands:	38	57	6
Coping with family commitments:	30	63	7
Coping with the stress of examinations:	23	63	13
Developing appropriate study skills (eg preparation and writing of essays):	23	64	14
Getting used to subjects not previously studied:	18	65	17
Remembering important parts of my course:	16	73	11
Keeping up with the academic level of the course:	16	72	12
Being able to grasp the meaning of specialised terms and concepts:	16	71	14
Coping with the financial costs of the course:	16	65	19
Coping with travel to and from college:	16	66	18
Developing confidence in my academic ability:	15	67	18
Coming to terms with the academic way of looking at things:	15	67	17
Getting used to a different approach to learning:	10	70	21
Coming to terms with changing beliefs and attitudes:	7	73	21
Making friends with fellow students:	4	66	30
Getting used to the college environment:	2	66	32

Owing to rounding, not all horizontal percentages sum to precisely 100.

We've reordered the 'difficulties' so that they're ranked on the basis of the proportion of respondents who found each item more difficult than expected. So you'll see that the numbers in the first of the three columns on the right hand side

2.1 *continued*

of the table systematically fall as you move from the top (at 54%) to the bottom (at 2%). We've also put them into three groups – we'll deal with each in turn.

But first let's be clear about what the table does and doesn't show. It doesn't show the levels of difficulty experienced by the students with the items shown. It does show the difficulties experienced by the students *compared with their initial expectations*. To some extent, this may reflect the fact that it's easier to assess the level of difficulty of some of the items than others.

Let's look first at the top group – the items that gave rise to more difficulty than expected.

	% of respondents who experienced more difficulty than expected
Finding the time to study:	54
Coping with competing demands of hobbies or other interests:	43
Organising my time in an efficient way:	39
Coping with job demands:	38
Coping with family commitments:	30

These are the 'big five'! The majority (54 per cent) of these part-time students encountered more difficulty in finding the time to study than they expected when they enrolled. Presumably, if they had more than 24 hours each day then they would also have found fewer difficulties in coping with the demands of other interests, their jobs and their family commitments. Almost 40 per cent saw the problem as one of time management ('organising my time in an efficient way'). For others it may be a question of becoming more aware of the time commitment and working through their priorities to discover where the time can be found.

Now let's go to the group at the bottom of the table. For all of the items below more students overestimated the difficulties than underestimated the difficulties. They include:

- Coping with the financial costs of the course
- Coping with travel to and from college
- Developing confidence in my academic ability
- Coming to terms with the academic way of looking at things

2.1 *continued*

- Getting used to a different approach to learning
- Coming to terms with changing beliefs and attitudes
- Making friends with fellow students
- Getting used to the college environment.

There may be items here that are of particular concern to you. If so, then you may be able to draw some comfort from these findings about your estimates of the level of difficulty that you will encounter from them.

That leaves the group of items in the middle of the table:

- Coping with the stress of examinations
- Developing appropriate study skills (eg preparation and writing of essays)
- Getting used to subjects not previously studied
- Remembering important parts of my course
- Keeping up with the academic level of the course
- Being able to grasp the meaning of specialised terms and concepts.

On balance more students underestimated the difficulties from each of these items than overestimated them. Do you now want to reflect a little more on how much difficulty each of these is likely to cause you? We won't explore these particular difficulties in the rest of this chapter but we'll pick most of them up in other parts of the book with suggestions for what you can do about each of them.

• •

Responses To SAQs, Chapter 3

Response 3.1

We said that you probably aren't aware of all the resources available to you to help you complete your course successfully. We asked a group of part-time students and a group of college staff what resources were available to a part-time student. Not surprisingly, there was a lot of overlap between the results. We've combined both lists, knocked out the duplications, and put them in some sort of order.

- **Home**

  People (eg cook dinner, look after the children, proof-read work, provide a sympathetic ear)
    - Partner
    - Friends (eg as babysitters)
    - Other significant persons (such as parents and other close relatives)
    - People that don't know anything about the course

  Things
    - Quiet space

- **College**

  People
    - Tutors: subject tutors and personal tutors
    - Other students, including students in previous years, full-time students (eg shared journeys, encouragement, other students' access to resources at work)
    - Library staff (usually very helpful)

  Things
    - College prospectus
    - Computer centre
    - Library: books that you can borrow, reference books, magazines, academic journals, photocopying facilities, catalogues, microfilm and microfiche facilities, videos,

3.1 *continued*

      on-line databases, newspaper archives, study areas, computer facilities
- Noticeboards
- Exam papers from previous years
- Student projects from previous years
- College support services

- **Work**

  People
  - The boss
  - Work colleagues

  Things
  - Finance
  - Work library resources
  - Photocopiers
  - Typing facilities
  - Equipment

- **Self**

  Experience, eg experience of any previous part-time study, maturity, greater assertiveness

  Abilities (natural), eg intelligence

  Abilities (developed), eg typing, driving, social skills, communication skills, numeracy, negotiating skills

  Attitudes, eg tenacity/stubbornness, patience, motivation

  Financial resources

  Health

- **Other**

  Bookshops

  Local public library

  Libraries of other academic institutions

  Open University programmes and publications

  Videos from Open University and other sources

  Computers

  Cassette recorder

  Radio and TV

Relaxation and relaxation amenities
Books
Feedback
Time (eg train journeys, in-car time for playing cassettes)
Local authority
Students' union at college and/or National Union of Students
Professional associations
Highlighter pens
Anybody else (if you ask).

Quite an impressive list isn't it? Compare the items on your own list of resources. Did you include anything that we haven't got on our list?

• •

Response 3.2
How about these?:

* college library (does your college have more than one library?)
* departmental office
* college reception/enquiries office
* student union
* student counselling service
* careers counselling service
* caretaker's office
* parking permits
* bookshop
* creche(?)
* bursary
* sports facilities
* college bar
* accomodation office
* health service
* computing centre
* educational development or learning resources centre
* refectory
* registry.

That's quite a list. And perhaps we've forgotten one or two (hopefully not important ones). Some of these offices and services have different names at different colleges. For example, the counselling service might be located within a unit called 'student services'. Don't be depressed if you missed many of these. The more that you didn't get, the more you've just learned.

• •

Response 3.3

We guess that you'll probably have ticked all the skills items. As we grow older we tend to acquire additional skills. Some of us acquire **technical skills,** like learning to drive, some of us acquire keyboard skills (keyboard skills are of increasing value in further and higher education with greater use being made of computers) and so on.

Some of us develop **conceptual skills** at work like planning the structure of reports, like managing projects and so on. Those of us who teach both full-time students and part-time students are often struck by how much better the part-timers are at preparing and writing reports. Conceptual skills are also developed in managing a home through such activities as planning outings and holidays, planning a house move and so on.

Some of us develop **social skills** like encouraging others, like handling people when they're being difficult. Certainly those of you who've brought up children or had a hand in bringing up children will have had a lot of practice developing valuable social skills. And if you've had to manage a home or manage projects at work or manage a hobby then you will have developed your **organisational skills.**

The point here is that learning is a natural by-product of living – learning from experience. Because you've done more living than you had at the time that you left school you'll have done a lot more learning. And the learning that you've done will be of great value to you in successfully completing a part-time course of study.

There's much talk in further and higher education circles nowadays about developing **transferable skills**. These are skills like the technical, conceptual, social and organisational skills mentioned above. They are called 'transferable' because they are not tied to any particular academic subject and they can be transferred between a wide range of applications. In particular, they can be transferred from a particular course of further or higher education on which they were developed to a range of other activities at work or in the home. But there's nothing to stop you reversing the process and using the personal transferable skills

3.3 *continued*

that you've developed at home and at work to get better results on your part-time course.

You might have ticked **commitment/motivation** to complete the course. We hope so – that's why we spent the first chapter helping you to sort out your reasons for doing your course. Some full-time students drift into their courses. Some speak about being on a 'conveyor belt' that takes them straight from school into a course of further or higher education to study whatever was their best subject at school. Often they haven't given too much consideration to whether it's what they really want to do. Some are accommodating parental assumptions that they will go on studying or parental pressures to study a particular subject or course. You're in a very different position. You've made a very conscious decision to do your course. And having got this far into this book you've carefully thought through why you want to do it, what the pitfalls could be and what your resources are to cope with them.

How about **money**? Did you tick that one? Well, you've probably got more money now but then you've probably also got more financial commitments. Much will depend upon the level of fees, and these vary greatly for part-time courses. In general, part-time courses are much less expensive than full-time courses. The annual course fees for most part-time courses are measured in hundreds of pounds whereas the annual course fees for most full-time courses are measured in thousands. Despite the maintenance grants available to many full-time students, most of them end each year with bank overdrafts and student loans!

In our research for this book we found that most of the part-time students experienced little difficulty in meeting the costs of taking their part-time course. One reason for this is that a large proportion of them got their employers to pay their fees and buy their books. However, for those who did experience financial difficulty, the drop-out rate was significantly higher.

How about your **self-confidence**? Are you more self-confident now than you were when you left school? It all depends on what you're doing. You may lack confidence in starting a part-time course of study. You're not sure what will be expected of you. You're not sure about your abilities. It's quite reasonable to have these doubts – most part-time students do. You can take comfort from the fact that by working through this book you are giving yourself the best chance that you can of succeeding. You're stacking the odds in your favour.

Do you think that you're more or less **intelligent** than you were when you left school? You might think that people's IQs stay the same throughout their adult

3.3 *continued*

lives.   On the other hand, you might think that intelligence declines because we lose brain cells with the passing of the years. The facts seem to be that intellectual growth continues until about the age of 40 when a plateau is reached which lasts until about 60. After this there is a slow decline until the mid-70s followed by a more rapid decline from then onwards. However, this decline only applies to the *speed* at which the brain works. Most intellectual activities are unrelated to speed and how no change between 20 and the mid-60s and little decline after that. So far the oldest Open University degree graduate is a woman of 92. In 1987 almost 3,500 people aged 60 or over studied at first-degree level with the Open University.

The real problem with age is that, having learned more, there may be more to unlearn in some circumstances. If you've learned 'bad habits' these can get in the way of learning. So, for instance, you may find it more difficult to learn how to touch type 'properly' if you are already pretty effective at one-finger typing.

Like the rest of your body, your head is made up of flesh, bones and blood. So what we now know about the benefits of physical fitness for your body applies also to your brain.

According to the psychologist Dr David Weeks, writing in *The Sunday Times,* (8 April 1990):

> In a study of the effects of physical exercise on the brain, middle-aged men who worked out for 4.5 hours a week were compared to a sedentary control group. The exercisers made major strides in their ability to process information coming at them first in successive sequences and then simultaneously. This represents a qualitative improvement, where the networks of brain cells are communicating with each other more efficiently.
>
> And more physical activity leads to better intellectual functioning even into old age. Good levels of alertness show up in faster reaction times and better recognition, and exercise promotes both. Men of 60 who exercise have reaction times comparable to men in their 20s.
>
> How much exercise do you need to do? The Edinburgh 'Super Young' project suggests that people begin to benefit when they have, on average, a brisk one-mile walk every other day. What sort of exercise you take must be a matter of choice and aptitude but the sooner the better.
>
> Physical exercise also makes you feel better: there are now many indications that people who exercise become less depressed, less hypochondriacal, develop more positive attitudes to life and improve their

3.3 *continued*

self-image. In a number of psychiatric institutes throughout America, Europe and the Third World, social jogging is now replacing heavy medication to relieve clinical depression. How? Exercise triggers the release of natural pain-killers, called beta-endomorphins, in the brain and body and in the brain this leads to mild elation and a sensation of gentle well-being. A jog a day keeps the psychiatrist away! If you find your sense of time slowing down, or outside events speeding by too fast, this could be an early sign of depression. And depression can interfere with both learning and the recall of knowledge.

Did you tick **energy?** Probably not. Compare the boisterous energy of toddlers with the more sedentary daily routines of most senior citizens. It seems reasonable to presume that there is a natural tendency for energy levels to fall with age. But against this there is the increased maturity that enables older people to channel their energies more effectively. Also, energy is related to commitment. The more committed and the more motivated that we feel about a course of action the more energy we are prepared to expend on it. And after working through Chapter 1 we hope that you feel sufficiently motivated to your course to focus your energies on it. Also, we've just been talking about the value of physical exercise in enhancing your mental powers and mental attitude; a little regular physical exercise will also raise your energy levels.

Information. Clearly you've got a lot more information in general than you had when you left school. You've lived longer so you've learned more. Have you got the right information? Some you'll get from this book. Some you'll get from documents such as your college or your course prospectus. Some you'll get from asking people: your tutors, fellow students and students in the year ahead of you. And you'll be much more effective in doing this if you spend time now making a note of the questions that you need to ask to get the information that will be helpful to you.

Support from others. Did you tick this one? We hope so because you are going to need support to successfully complete a part-time course. This is a continuing theme of this book. If you didn't tick it don't worry – with the social skills that you've developed since leaving school you should be able to develop the sort of support network that you'll need. Later on in this chapter we'll look at what sort of support you may need and we'll give you an opportunity to sort out how you can get it.

Study skills. You probably didn't tick this one. School may have been a long while ago and you may have forgotten how to study. Never mind, the study skills of most school leavers leave much to be desired. Perhaps you've forgotten how to do it wrong! In this case it may be the school leavers who have the bad habits to cope with rather than you. Best of all, most of the rest of this book is devoted to improving your study skills.

Time. We guess you didn't tick this one! Time is, of course, the main resource that part-time students are short of. Still we hope that you'll now agree that you have other resources that will compensate for this.

• •

Response 3.4

We hope that you're surprised at how many skills you've developed since you left school. Many of these skills will be valuable to you as a part-time student. The list is long but it's not exhaustive. We're sure that there are other skills that you've developed since you've left school that will help you to be successful on your course.

• •

Response 3.5

Now you know why we called these questions self-analysis questions. It's difficult for us to comment on your choices as only you know what sort of part-time course you are pursuing. We'd like to reiterate, however, that in different contexts they can all be of value. The important thing is that you clarify your strengths and your personal assets as they are key resources in successfully completing your part-time degree course.

• •

Response 3.6

When people answer this SAQ many find that their support network is less well developed than they thought. Was that your experience? Did you find more gaps than you feel comfortable with? Do you need to strengthen your support network? Did you find the same name(s) recurring too often? If so, is this a realistic level of support to expect from them? Do you need to widen your support network?

If you need to strengthen your support network then complete the following:

3.6 *continued*

What actions will I take?

At work:

Away from work

Responses To SAQs, Chapter 4

Response 4.1
Whoever you chose as your competent person, we think that the things you wrote as evidence of their competence will be roughly as follows:

- things they can do
- things they have done
- skills they demonstrate
- qualifications they may have obtained.

We expect you'll have found that you can't really describe a competent person except in terms of things like those listed above. So this leads us to a definition of competence along the lines of:

can do........ statements
or *have done*..........statements.

Response 4.2
The opposite of competence is incompetence of course – or is it? We'd like to challenge that for the moment, and ask you to think of it as *un*competence. The trouble with the word 'incompetence' is that we've all got negative associations towards it – involving thoughts like 'idiot', 'buffoon', 'thick as two short planks' and so on.

Uncompetence is a lot simpler and kinder, and may be simply *can't yet do* rather than *can't do*. There are other manifestations of uncompetence, which could cover 'don't *want* to do', 'don't *need* to do' and even '*won't* do'.

Response 4.3
We guess you may have been surprised how easy it is to find things that belong in the target box – conscious competences. You've probably got lots more things

you could add to this box. Many will turn out to be highly relevant to the success of your studies. More about this later.

•••

Response 4.4

We could all fill pages with conscious uncompetences! However, most things are perfectly all right staying where they are in this box. It's only some of the 'can't yet do' things which may need moving towards your target box. It's for those that we called the conscious uncompetence box the transit box.

Do you feel better about some of the things you can't do, by splitting them up into 'don't need to do' and 'don't want to do' and so on? It's quite common for people to feel inferior about not being able to do something – then it turns out that there's absolutely no need to do it! There's no reason why we should all be competent at everything! Life would be very dull!

Probably, you found that there aren't all that many 'can't yet do' things – not as many as you may have expected. So your agenda of turning these into 'can do' things is not as daunting as you may have thought.

•••

Response 4.5

Let's look at some of the things that Jenny can do – but perhaps doesn't really know she can do.

She can manage a range of demands efficiently. She's already doing this regarding home, children and her present job. She'll be better able to fit in more extra time for her studies than many a person who does far less. ('If you want a job done well, give it to a busy person' is a proverb with a lot of truth behind it.)

She has motivation – but probably as an unconscious competence. She wants a more interesting career, and sees studying as her passport to better things. This motivation is a strong factor in guaranteeing her success – many capable people lack such a vital ingredient.

You may have thought of more competences than these: you may know Jenny better than we do.

•••

Response 4.6

Sadly, we can't be with you to talk to you about the SWOT analysis you've just done! We wish we could. However, you may well have someone else who could give you comments about it – or, better, several other people. It's amazing how helpful it is to discuss these analyses with other people who have done the same thing.

In case you're on your own, we'll give you some comments to help you make the most of the analysis you did.

Strengths: it's good to have a list of these. They help keep your spirits up, and help you fight occasional feelings of despair – we all get them now and then! Look again at each of the strengths you listed, and this time ask yourself 'How best can I harness this strength to help make my studying successful?' Jot down comments here and there to remind you how you intend to use your strengths.

Weaknesses: Look again through any things you listed in this box, and write 'doesn't matter' against any that haven't got a direct bearing on your immediate studies. Don't regard any weaknesses that remain as 'can't do' – make them clearly 'can't *yet* do'. In fact, why not be bold and cross out the word 'weaknesses' and substitute 'strengths not yet developed'. These can be part of your agenda for progress (far better than not having any plan of action).

Opportunities: it could be worth you writing these out big on a large sheet of paper and sticking them up on a wall! It's good to have some convincing answers on those days that you'll ask yourself 'Why am I doing all this?' Don't forget to add to the opportunities. Every time you meet a difficult task, regard it as an opportunity to develop further competences.

Threats: 'Know thy enemy' is a proverb that was around even before we started our studies! It's still good advice. If you face the things that could stop you, you can prepare to make sure they *don't* stop you. You can make plans to avoid some threats, to tackle others head on, and so on. If you're really ambitious in your SWOT analysis, you can simply draw arrows from each threat, moving it into the opportunity box. See what we mean? A threat provides you with an opportunity to conquer it or make it redundant.

●●

Responses To SAQs, Chapter 5

Response 5.1

Please check *your* ways of finding time for studying against the comments we've made below.

I make precise plans – for example Thursday evenings 2000–2130, Saturdays 1015–1230 etc. You're well disciplined. If this works for you – great. But does it really? Ask yourself the following questions:

* During your carefully planned study sessions, do you sometimes catch yourself thinking about all sorts of other things?
* Does your schedule become your excuse for not trying to study at other times?

I hate plans. I work when the mood takes me. This is perfectly all right if you can answer 'yes' at any time to one simple question – 'Am I doing sufficient work?' (We'll look at how you can tell whether you're doing sufficient work in Chapters 7 and 10).

I just can't work during the week – I've no time. I can however get some longish spells of work fitted in to the average weekend. People studying part time often work this way. The weekend may indeed be the only time you can find a solid two-hour spell or two. But friends may be neglected, family may become resentful. And anyway, weekends aren't as long as you hope they will be. It sometimes takes all of Saturday to recover from the week, and most of Sunday to recover from Saturday! And perhaps it takes half a day to get ready to get started? Don't rely on weekends for miracles. And is a two-hour spell a good idea at all? We'll discuss this soon.

I tend to do a bit of studying whenever there's nothing else crying out to be done. That's good – or at least it may be good. The problem can be that there *always* seems to be something else crying out to be done. Studying then gets postponed – and postponed again. Are these other things real or are they cunning excuses for not starting studying? Only you can tell. Be honest with yourself.

I travel around quite a lot, and use some of this time for studying. We were thinking of trains, planes and buses, not driving – please don't study as you drive (except for some things we'll mention in Chapter 6)! If you do spend quite some time travelling or commuting, you may find you can do some study activities as you go.

When I've a lot to do, I set the alarm one hour earlier, and put in an hour before the day really starts. We think this is a splendid idea – well done. We're like this too. That's how we've made the time to write this book! There are some penalties though – your partner may get sick of you nodding off during the 6 o'clock evening news. Seriously though, even if you're not at all a morning person you may surprise yourself by how well you remember things you study early in the day.

My life is full – I just don't know where I'm going to find any time for studying! Don't worry, there should be plenty of ideas in this chapter (and some more in Chapter 6) which will help you.

I've not ticked *any* of these – I'm different. As long as your way leads to a resounding 'yes' to the question 'Are you doing sufficient studying?' you're doing just fine doing it your way.

• •

Response 5.2

We can't comment on exactly what you put as your sample time audit, but we can help you analyse it for yourself. We'd like you to do three things with your audit, as follows. It would help if you have pens or pencils of three colours (if not, use three different kinds of shading – diagonal/vertical/horizontal etc).

Analysing your time audit
First: in colour 1, shade in all the areas of your audit which are essential as they stand. This will include eating, sleeping, travelling times perhaps, time at your job, maybe some essential family/friends commitments, and so on. You be the judge. Shade in these areas now, then return to this page and read on.

Second: in colour 2, shade in those areas of your audit which could be regarded as negotiable. These could include watching TV, simply relaxing, reading the paper, breaks in your job hours, chatting time, some family/friends commitments. Do this now, then read on below....

By now, your 24-hour day will be well shaded. Any white areas are possible study time. Some of your 'negotiable' time may be possible study time too. Even some of your 'essentials' time could be used for study – maybe half an hour less sleep, or a slightly quicker dinner. Now to the final step.

Third: use colour 3 to shade in *some* of the time you could use for studying. Some of this will be white space on your audit, but other study times may be gained by using some of your 'negotiable' time, and even trimming your 'essentials' time a little here and there. But don't shade in all the potential study time, just a reasonable amount – maybe a third or a half of the total possible. Then return to this response for the remainder of our discussion.

Discussion

You may have been surprised by how much time you have – even if you chose a typically busy day with many hours earning your living. On the other hand, you may be becoming alarmed that there are so many 'essentials' in your schedule that you may not have enough time for studying. In this case, don't panic – there's a lot you can do to use the little time you have as efficiently as possible.

Please rejoin the text again, and we'll follow this up.

• •

Response 5.3

3 hours: sometimes there will be things you need to do which need three hours – but not often. The danger with a long study period is that there aren't going to be many of them. You may wait a long time before you get a solid three-hour spell when you can get down to it.

2 hours: this is quite a long time. There aren't going to be many spare two-hour slots in your busy life. If you have them, of course *use* them. But maybe experiment with some shorter times too.

1 hour: it's surprising how much can be done in an hour. Make good use of those hours. But perhaps there are some shorter spells of time in your life, too, that you could also put to good use?

30 minutes: this is a good choice. Even in a long spell of work, most of the real work may get done in the first half-hour or the last half-hour. Also, there are exactly twice as many half-hours in the week as there are hours (and six times as many as there are three-hour spells!). So you shouldn't have too long to wait before you can squeeze in half an hour's studying.

15 minutes: an even better choice perhaps (see our comments for 30 minutes above). Of course, you have to get yourself conditioned to jump-starting if you're going to get maximum value out of short bits of time. We'll look at ways of jump-starting in Chapter 7.

Something else? If you wrote something here, hopefully it was less than 15 minutes rather than more than three hours! Or possibly something along the lines of 'whatever time is available' or 'it all depends on the task in hand'. It is quite remarkable how effective the odd few minutes here and there can be, if you know how best to use them. (More about this later.)

• •

Response 5.4

People want me to do other things. Here are some ways of preventing this:

- Set aside – and tell other people about – times when you must not be disturbed. The more regular your routine, the easier it is for them to learn not to disturb you at these times

- Plan time to be with these other people as well

- Don't be afraid to say *no* – gently but firmly.

The TV tempts me away from studying. Ways of preventing this are:

- Don't have one! (but we don't expect everyone to take us up on this!)

- Work miles away from the TV!

5.4 *continued*

- Try to watch it after rather than before your study sessions – make watching TV a reward for study you've done

- See if you can get conditioned (as many schoolkids now are) to having the TV on and taking not a blind bit of notice of it! It can become like 'wallpaper' and many people can study with it as an unnoticed background. (Don't tell the advertisers we said this or we could be sued for millions!) But be aware that some activities are easier to do with the TV on than others

- Sort out well in advance which programmes you particularly want to see, and those you are prepared to sacrifice. This way you're less likely to turn on the TV on the offchance that something interesting is on.

- If you've got a video recorder, *record* all of your favourite programmes, but only *watch* them after you've done some studying. Turn the distraction into a rewards system.

Doing household jobs and duties. Here are some ways around this:

- Schedule times to do such duties – well away from your normal study times

- Delegate some of these. If you've got kids they may be very willing to take some on – at a price!

- Hold back the urge! Do all the jobs really need doing? Ask yourself: 'Am I just putting-off working?'

Boredom or exhaustion. The in-phrase is 'burn-out'. Burn-out is highly contagious. Many people catch it by just reading about it. Worrying about it is the main cause of getting it. Studying (gently) can be one of the best cures! The following ideas may help:

- Get interested in your studies – look back at your reasons for studying

- Set yourself satisfying but realistic targets. Don't expect miracles!

- Think of taking a break and getting some exercise.

5.4 *continued*

Distractions from neighbours or family. There are ways around this:

- Do some of your studying regularly in a spot away from such distractions if you can

- Warn others when you'll be working, and ask for their cooperation

- Don't exclude family or close friends. Think of ways they can get involved in your studies – for example asking you to explain things to them, or testing you on lists of questions you're practising with.

My natural tendency to put things off. Well, at least you're honest. The following may help you:

- Work on your motivation: if you can get to the stage of wanting to study, rather than just feeling you ought to study, you'll have less trouble with procrastination. Keep reminding yourself what's in it for you. Look forward to the benefits that come with success. Keep your long-term aims in sight

- Let other people know your targets – and your problem! The fact that someone will ask you 'Did you do that assignment you talked about yesterday?' is a strong motivator!

I get discouraged by the amount of work. There are ways around this:

- Make sure you're giving yourself realistic targets – you may be aiming too high

- Do your studying in small chunks; your confidence will build as you complete each step

- Build in lots of breaks to keep fresh.

● ●

Responses To SAQs, Chapter 6

Response 6.1

I'll have to sort out a suitable study area at home. You're in good company. Most part-time students when first starting to study this way need to sort out something at home. But be careful! It's possible to spend a long time sorting out things at home, rather than actually getting some learning under way.

I've no problem, I've already got a good place for studying at home. Congratulations – you're lucky. That said, there are dangers to be avoided. Will your place at home be the only place you'll use for studying?

I'll have to go out to study, maybe to a library or some such place. If you're in this position, when you get to the library you may indeed work efficiently. But will you actually get there when there's a force eight gale blowing, or a foot of snow, or if you've got a bit of a cough? And how much time, energy and money will you spend travelling to and from your place of study?

I'll be doing much of my studying at work, where I have a suitable place. This is fine if it works. The problem is that it may not be as easy to get on as you think. People come and talk to you. When you're labouring with a hard bit it's tempting for you to escape and do something else. And you'll probably only be able to use the place at particular times.

Help! I really don't know where I'm going to find space to do my learning. Well, if you've read the rest of the responses we gave above, you'll have noticed that even the best places have dangers associated with them. In fact, it's more useful if you can do some studying in *less-than-ideal* circumstances, than to search endlessly for the ideal place. What's even more important is that you study efficiently. (More of that later.) It's only too easy to sit in the best study in the world and daydream!

••

Response 6.2

We've found that the main danger in having a good place to study is what happens when you're not there!

What happens? Do you use the fact that you're not in your ideal place as a reason not to bother trying to study? 'I'll wait till I get back to where I can really make progress' you may say. Is that a reason for not doing some work? We think it's an excuse!

• •

Response 6.3

This time, we can't comment on what you wrote. But we can add a suggestion: in the next seven days, do something related to your studies in each of the places you chose. Then decide what worked and what didn't.

• •

Responses To SAQs, Chapter 7

Response 7.1

Don't worry if you ticked all of the options! Most people do. At least until they've taken on board some of the suggestions in this chapter.

If you only ticked some of them, good – you've already solved some of the problems that cause studying to be inefficient.

If you didn't tick any of these, either you're already highly organised in the way you go about studying – or you're kidding yourself! (Only you can tell.)

• •

Response 7.2

	work	**WORK**
1 Writing essays	√	
2 Writing reports	√	
3 Making summaries		√
4 Preparing a seminar	√	
5 Reading round the subject	√	
6 Making lists of questions		√
7 Rewriting lecture notes	√	
8 Practising answering questions		√
9 Making essay plans		√
10 Doing literature searches	√	
11 Doing set homework	√	
12 Discussing topics with other students		

Did your answer agree with ours? The problem with so many of the things we described as work is that although you're very busy while you're doing them, not very much sticks in your brain after you've finished them. We've explained briefly below why we categorised the dozen things as above.

Notes

1   Writing essays: takes a lot of time, not always a lot of learning.

7.2 *continued*

2 Writing reports: takes a lot of putting together. Relatively short bursts of real learning.

3 Making summaries of things: very active way of working, sorting out priorities. High learning payoff.

4 Preparing a seminar: a lot of routine searching and organising – not that much real learning.

5 Reading round the subject: useful, good for the mind but dangerously unproductive! Your time is precious – regard such reading as a luxury for *after* the real work is done.

6 Making lists of questions: high learning payoff. You can test yourself against these lists of questions. More about this soon.

7 Rewriting lecture notes: low learning payoff. You can easily become a human photocopier, writing without thinking. Making summaries has much higher learning payoff and forces you to *think*.

8 Practising answering questions: high learning payoff – good practice for what you'll need to be good at sooner or later.

9 Making essay plans: this can have a high learning payoff, as essay plans can be made quickly and actively: it's putting the essay together that's slow. So you can plan dozens of essays, but only do those you need or want to.

10 Doing literature searches: often necessary, but low learning payoff. You spend more time tracking down the bit you want than actively using it having found it!

11 Doing set homework: necessary maybe, but not necessarily high learning payoff. Checking you can still do it four weeks later has higher learning payoff.

12 Discussing topics with other students: this can have the highest learning payoff. It involves working actively.

Response 7.3

The other difference we had in mind was: 'work' tends to be 'solicited'. In other words your lecturers and tutors give it to you to do. This is fine of course, as long as it's not what you spend all your time doing.

'**WORK**' tends to be 'unsolicited.' In other words things *you* decide to do. The danger is that although these activities have high learning payoff, you're too busy trying to keep up with the solicited work, and don't get started on the unsolicited variety.

•••

Response 7.4

Here's what we think of these strategies.

Every time after doing some work (**essays, reports, and so on**) **do 15 minutes of WORK.** Great if you can do it! But can you? Isn't there a danger of saying 'Blow it, I've done enough today' after finishing off the routine work? Also, your mind will be tired, and even if you do manage to fit in some **WORK** it probably won't be of the highest quality.

Build in study periods deliberately for WORK and keep routine work **for other times.** This could be very effective and worth aiming for, but it takes strong will-power. What if other things are crying out to be done? Will you still have the strength to do what after all is unsolicited work? Perhaps the next response is safer.

Do 15 minutes of WORK every time before you settle down to do work **of the more routine variety.** This really does work (excuse the pun!). The routine work may be 15 minutes later than it would otherwise have been but that isn't going to seriously damage it! The important thing about this strategy is that it's a way of regularly getting some of the real work done as well. Also, you're doing the high-payoff variety before your brain gets tired.

Better still: also spend an extra five minutes after finishing the routine work to quickly review the things you did in that first 15 minutes.

•••

Response 7.5

Of course, there's no reason why your egg should look anything like ours! Nevertheless, here are ours:

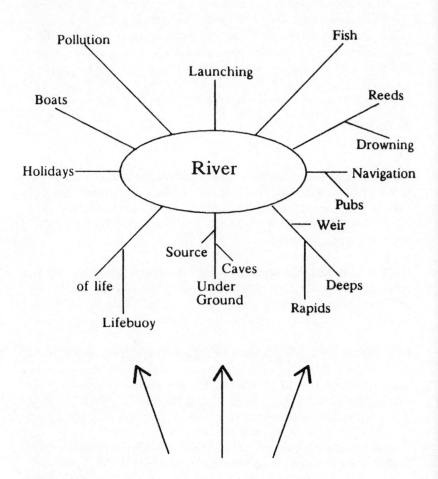

Figure R7.1 *River 'egg'*

But may not the 'branches' be counter-productive in the long run? Next, look at some examples without branches – why may they be better?

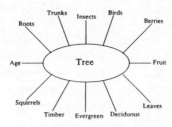

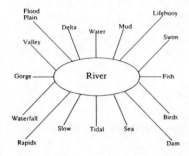

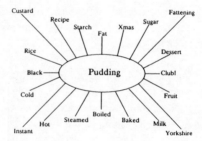

Figure R7.2 *Tree, river and pudding 'eggs'*

Response 7.6

We think you should assemble the middle first. This will contain just about all the material in your essay, arranged carefully in the most logical order. (This is why it's handy to have separate paragraphs on separate bits of paper – or of course on a word processor.)

We think that secondly you should draft your conclusions. Any essay is judged quite a lot on how well it comes to conclusions. The conclusions need to address whatever the title asked for (there are of course all sorts of titles – and all sorts of ways of bringing essays to a good conclusion). The important thing is to make sure that the essay doesn't just stop.

Finally, we recommend you write your introduction. Seems odd? Not really: the introduction is very important. It colours the way the whole of your essay will be regarded. Your essay needs to live up to the promise of its introduction. What better way than to write the introduction when you know exactly what the essay contains – and what conclusions you reached?

Do you see the logic of working on middle, then end, then finally the beginning? We think the advice applies equally well to reports, dissertations, and in fact just about any piece of written work that you're likely to be asked to produce.

● ●

Response 7.7

Here are four ways (not in particular order) which help avoid 'reading limbo'.

- Read selectively. Use the index and contents pages to track down exactly which bits you really need to read

- Use a pen or pencil or highlighter. Make notes, highlight important parts – above all, jot down key points to remember. Highlighting by itself is just a bit too passive!

- Write questions. Jot down, in question form, things you think it's important to learn from what you read. Then, a day or two later, test yourself on your questions. Keep the answers going through your mind, don't let them evaporate

- Go back to the most important passages again and again. The more often you've thought about something, the better you're going to understand it. Difficult things may take several times before your mind really begins to master them.

- If you thought of some further ways of avoiding 'reading limbo', all the better – add our ways to yours and you're even better off.

● ●

Responses To SAQs, Chapter 8

Response 8.1

If you said either of the following things then congratulate yourself because they're both true:

- All three can contribute to being successful on your course
- All three can help you to learn and memorise your course material.

However, they also have two other things in common:

- They are all passive ways of learning
- If these are all that you do then you are severely limiting your chances of being as successful on your course as you could be.

If you said either or both of these points, well done – you're on our wavelength already.

....

Response 8.2

Were you surprised how many options we gave you? Were you surprised at the variety of the things we listed? Were you surprised at how many you ticked as things that might appeal to you?

Even if you only ticked half a dozen of the options, you have selected some different learning experiences which can bring productivity and interest to your studies.

....

Response 8.3

We hope you found it useful to make decisions about which of the active learning options you will start experimenting with.

Of course, you can build in some of the things you didn't tick at all. Any time. Use the list as a toolshop, and add to your personal toolkit as often as you like.

• •

Response 8.4

You may have surprised yourself with how many of those activities can be done
with friends. They may turn out quite differently: two minds are better than one,
and so on.

Of course, you can do some of them on your own first, then repeat them with
friends. There are all sorts of possibilities.

• •

Response 8.5

You may already have found that your fellow students are a powerful resource to
you – and you to them. Working 'privately' is all right for some things, but many
learning activities are more productive and stimulating when done with other
people. You'll soon find out who best to work with: maybe a variety of friends for
a variety of tasks. Or maybe one or two people you work closely with for a whole
range of tasks.

• •

Responses To SAQs, Chapter 9

Response 9.1

I feel a bit threatened – especially when faced with the prospect of handing in work for assessment. This feeling is quite normal. It's important to realise that it's not you that will be assessed – it's your work. The main purpose of coursework assessments is to give you some idea of how you're doing. The most important aspect of coursework is what you do with the feedback you get. More about this in Chapter 10.

I get a bit impatient when the tutor is explaining to the group things I already know. Who doesn't? Maybe, however, the tutor doesn't know you already know it. This will be compounded if you just sit there quietly and say nothing. One way or another, show that you know it – nodding, smiling, adding comments of your own when you get the chance ... the tutor will soon get the message that there's no point in expounding something that most people already know.

I don't like asking questions – I'm afraid I may look silly! Even a simple question can loom very large until you know the answer. The chances are that if you don't know the answer, other people don't know it either. You would be doing the whole group a service by asking the question. If you still don't want to ask, at least write the question down – there are other ways of finding the answer. If you don't either ask it or write it down, you're likely to forget what the question was. Then you'll never find the answer.

Sometimes there's a tutor I just don't like – and I find it difficult to 'warm' to his or her subject. This is perfectly natural. None of us likes everyone equally. You may occasionally get a tutor who really raises your hackles. But you don't have to *like* this person – all you need to do is to master the subject. Be aware that you can still learn from such people even if you don't like them. You may, however, choose to be more self-directed in your learning of the subject, relying on other sources rather than just the tutor. But still turn up for sessions so that you can glean information that will be useful to you.

I really look forward to class sessions – there's a great atmosphere and I enjoy them. This is the hallmark of a good tutor and also of a good group! Atmosphere comes from both sides. Even the best of tutors can't make magic if most people in the group are cold and withdrawn. When you and the tutor create classes with a great atmosphere, learning comes easily.

So-and-so is a really splendid tutor – I could learn anything from this tutor. You may be lucky enough to meet such an individual. You may indeed be able to ask such a person questions from other subject areas where you haven't got a good tutor. (Don't worry, any brilliant tutor is used to being asked all sorts of questions.) One thing to watch: be careful that the splendid tutor doesn't take up too much of your time, energy and enthusiasm – you'll still need to learn the rest of your subjects well enough to pass the course.

Some of the tutors make me feel a bit like being back at school, and I don't like that. Try to work out why you feel you are back at school. Perhaps you're sitting in rows; a square or a circle may be less formal. Perhaps someone who comes in a bit late gets dirty looks; best be on time anyway. Perhaps communication is a bit too one-way; a few well considered questions from the floor may break the ice. Perhaps the tutor is actually a bit afraid of the group; can *you* make the tutor feel a bit more relaxed?

• •

Response 9.2

Here are our thoughts on the ways typical tutors may react to these various ways of being asked questions.

Ask questions in the middle of one of your sessions. This could be unwelcome, especially if the tutor doesn't readily know the answer, or if time is short and there's a lot to be done in the session. Questions are much more likely to be welcome in a seminar or tutorial.

Come up to you at the end of the session, and ask questions. This is all right if the tutor doesn't have to be somewhere else in five minutes – for example, another class.

Give you a note saying 'when you've got time, could you glance at these questions, and come back to me with some answers?' This is fine. It allows the tutor the freedom to deal with the questions when time is available, and the chance to research the answers to them.

Send you a note along the same lines as above. This is also fine; it allows the tutor the same freedoms as the previous example. However, it does have the disadvantage that the tutor may not be able to associate the face with the questions. It's useful for tutors to know which student asked a particular question.

Ring you up at work during the day. Part-time students may indeed need to use the phone to contact tutors now and then. However, if the tutor is already teaching or talking with colleagues then phone interruptions may occasionally be unwelcome.

Ring you up at home during the weekend. *Some* tutors – you'll know the sort – invite such calls. Sadly, there aren't many such. Most will want to keep their home life separate from their work.

Ask Mrs Johnston – a colleague of yours who seems less busy – instead of asking you. This sort of thing can work, but it can backfire. What if Mrs Johnston starts saying 'All Mr Bloggs's students keep coming asking me questions'!

Make an appointment with you to come and see you at a time suitable for both of you. This is a good way out, especially if the tutor is alerted to exactly what the questions (or problems) are.

● ●

Response 9.3

Here are some questions about a forthcoming exam which would normally be accepted as 'reasonable' ones:

- How long is the paper – two or three hours?
- Is the paper divided into sections, with (for example) three questions to be attempted from section A, two from section B and so on?
- Will there be any compulsory questions – or does the paper give a completely free choice?

- Is the choice any five out or eight questions? Or five out of 12? (How would you prepare differently for those two papers?)
- Where can I find some specimen or past papers to practise with?
- Will the exam be just on what we've done this year, or may it involve things we studied previously?

Questions like these are better than just 'Can you tell us about the structure of the exam?' It's clearer what specific information you want and it's harder for any tutor not to answer such specific questions. Be careful not to make the tutor feel 'grilled' or he or she may get defensive. One step at a time!

Our response has dealt with questions about exams. You can easily extend the ideas to questions about coursework assessment, projects and so on.

• •

Response 9.4

Now let's have a look at those statements and find out if you've got any misconceptions that might trip you up.

1 **Most college tutors receive training in how to teach.** Until recently, very few tutors received any real training in teaching. Tutors are still mostly appointed on the basis of their subject expertise. They are still sometimes thrown into teaching at the deep end, without any advice on such things as how to give lectures or how to mark coursework. This leads them to base their teaching methods on what they experienced when they were students (which may have been good or bad) and on trial and error. This can lead to problems when they come to use newer technologies which weren't around when they were students. For example, a new tutor who has mastered the art of producing impressive overhead transparencies using a desk-top publishing system may whiz them on and off the projector at a rate that is far too fast for you to note down the things you wish to from each slide. It's important that you give your tutors feedback on anything like this – or they'll never even know there's a problem. Providing good feedback to your tutors is an important part of getting better results from them.

In recent years, the Staff and Educational Development Association (SEDA) has set up a 'Teacher Accreditation Scheme' for staff in universities in the UK. Universities which participate in this scheme help

9.4 *continued*

staff (particularly new staff) to acquire and demonstrate a broad set of competences to do with teaching, course design and assessing. We think you'll approve of the difference when you're taught by a SEDA-accredited tutor!

2 **The main job of college tutors is to teach.** Teaching is the main rationale of most academic institutions. This does not mean that tutors spend most of their time doing face-to-face teaching. This is the visible part of a tutor's job – the exposed part of the iceberg. It is directly supported by activities such as writing lectures, planning and preparing classes, setting coursework and examinations and marking them.

In addition, your tutors will (one hopes) see education as a continuing process for themselves as well as for you. So they'll spend considerable time reading, if only to keep up to date in their subject.

Beyond this, there is a range of activities that they're expected to undertake. These may include:

- research
- administration
- attending courses (eg doing a higher degree part time themselves)
- writing books
- attending conferences
- course development
- attending meetings and sitting on committees.

By focusing only on the face-to-face teaching part, the job of a tutor appears to be relaxed, even leisurely. For most college tutors the reality is quite different. So don't be offended or surprised if they are sometimes less willing to spend time chatting with you than you would like.

3 **College tutors get promotion on the basis of how well they perform as teachers.** Do you want to get promotion in your job? As a person doing a part-time course of study, there's a better than average chance that you do. Many college tutors are ambitious too. Colleges use various criteria in promoting academic staff – especially competent teaching, research and administration. Unfortunately, teaching competence is difficult to measure

9.4 *continued*

and not very visible. Consequently, more emphasis tends to be placed on research record and willingness to share the load of administration than teaching ability.

We've mentioned this because you may encounter an ambitious tutor who is more interested in researching and publishing than in teaching.

4   **Nearly all your tutors will give interesting lectures.** You'll be very lucky if all do! No tutor sets out to give boring lectures, any more than anyone sets out to be a bore. All tutors would all prefer to give classes that stimulate and motivate you. You're very likely to encounter on your course tutors who do stimulate you and you're also very likely to encounter some whose lectures you find uninteresting. Don't make the mistake of inferring that you can't learn from a tutor who is not an entertainer. It's easy to learn from a good tutor; it takes a good student to learn from a poor tutor. There may be times to say to yourself: 'This is not the tutor that I would have chosen for this course but what can I learn from this person anyway?'

5   **Your tutors will have done a lot of preparation for your classes.** Most of your tutors will have done a lot of preparation for your classes. Often, much more than is apparent. However, sometimes other personal and work commitments get in the way. Sometimes, even a well-planned class won't always work out as well as the tutor planned. And occasionally some tutors may get so confident about a class that they do little preparation for it.

6   **Your tutors will take a personal interest in you.** Some of your tutors will want to get to know you as a person and will devote time to doing just that. Many of the staff who teach on part-time courses do so because they like teaching more mature people, admire the tenacity of part-time students and feel a commitment to widening access to further and higher education. Others do it with some reluctance because it involves teaching at unpopular times and just because it's on their teaching timetable. Some tutors have such busy professional lives that they have less time to spend with their students than they would like (some tutors have such busy professional lives that they have less time to spend with their *families* than they would like!). Some tutors teach hundreds of different students each week and don't want to have favourites. Some tutors are shy outside of the classroom. Some are

9.4 *continued*

private people who prefer to relate to their students through their subject rather than becoming personally involved.

In our research for this book we found, however, that most students enjoyed good relationships with their tutors. About 90 per cent reported that their college tutors were very supportive or generally supportive. Since writing the first edition of this book, things have changed in that tutors are under much more pressure, and often have to deal with classes containing many more students than just a few years ago. Sadly, this means that if you're in a large class, the possibility of even the most willing tutor getting to know each student is reduced.

7   **Your tutors will have little interest in you personally and will resent being bothered about your difficulties.** If you have difficulties in a subject, most tutors would prefer you to seek advice or assistance from them rather than keeping quiet about it. Some students are overawed by tutors who may be called 'professor' or 'doctor'. Most tutors enjoy talking with students who have a genuine wish to learn. The difficulty for many part-time students – especially those who attend classes on the basis of evening only – is lack of time. When they're in college they are scheduled to attend classes. And when they're not attending classes they may have difficulty making contact with the tutors whose assistance they need, since tutors tend not to stay around college in the evening when they aren't teaching. Don't be afraid to telephone the college and arrange an appointment. Also, don't forget that there are other sources of help besides tutors. Colleges normally have Student Counsellors. Sometimes, there will be such a Counsellor specialising in academic matters – for example, guidance on what choices to make when courses provide options.

8   **College tutors want students to challenge all ideas and give their own viewpoints in class.** Some tutors will welcome useful contributions from students. A small minority will have little interest in students' views. Many will feel that they have only a limited time to present large amounts of information. They may discourage student 'interruptions'. This is likely to be a particular problem if they are expected to 'get through' the same amount of material as they cover in more time with the full-time students. For them, completing the syllabus will be more important than encouraging students to express their opinions. In general, your contributions will be more welcome in seminars or tutorials than in formal lectures.

9.4 *continued*

9 **University and college tutors don't want you to think for yourself, they want you simply to record everything that they say and regurgitate it in examinations.** The aims of most tutors are two-fold: to get you to understand the main concepts and theories in their field and to get you to think for yourself. So the fact that you learn the course material shouldn't stop you from questioning the assumptions and conclusions.

10 **College tutors are friendly people.** Some are, some aren't. College tutors are human beings! Friendliness is probably distributed across college tutors in about the same proportion as it is in the population at large. That means that it's entirely possible that at some stage on your course you will encounter a grouch who you regard as pretty unfriendly. However, the question 'Does this person like me?' is likely to be less productive for you to ask than 'Does this person know enough about the subject to be a resource for me to learn about the subject?'

11 **You can't teach a subject well if you haven't had first-hand experience.** There is no doubt that first-hand experience is helpful. Many people with first-hand experience don't know how to teach what they can do well. Can you swim or ride a bike? If you answered yes to either or both, have you ever tried to teach someone how to swim or how to ride a bike? Just because you can do it doesn't mean that you're good at teaching it.

On the other hand, it's not essential to have first-hand experience to be able to teach effectively. You don't need to have been there to teach history well. (If you did then there wouldn't be many good teachers of *ancient* history!) You can learn about abnormal psychology from someone who isn't abnormal. You can learn useful ideas about business from someone who has never run a business. 'What first-hand experience does this tutor have?' can be a relevant question but a much more useful question is 'How well does this tutor teach?'

12 **College tutors are able to answer all your questions on their subject.** It's reassuring when your tutor can answer all your questions. But perhaps it's an indication that your tutor finds it difficult to admit that he or she doesn't know. Or perhaps the level of the course is so low that you aren't being exposed to difficult ideas. If you're doing a demanding course, your tutor is honest or your questins are good ones, it's likely that sometimes your

tutor will not know the answer. Then if you're lucky he or she will say so and suggest ways that you can find out the answer.

• •

Response 9.5

Tell your tutor after the class that you liked the lecture. This is well worth doing as it reinforces good behaviour by your tutor. You may think that it's not your place to compliment tutors or that your tutor will think that you're 'creeping'. If you're sincere, almost all lecturers would be lifted by the fact that you've taken the time to express your appreciation. It's only creeping if you're not sincere – and that would probably be pretty apparent.

Tell your tutor the next time that you see him or her in the corridor that you liked the lecture. This is also worth doing but it's not as good as doing it immediately after the lecture. The quicker you reward the behaviour that you want to encourage the more effective is the reward.

Tell your tutor straight after the class what you liked about the lecture. This is better still as you're rewarding quickly and you're being specific about the behaviour that you want to encourage. The more specific that you are, the better the feedback. This is like when you get some coursework marked and the tutor's comment at the end is just 'good'. You get some feedback about how you're doing and you may feel motivated by knowing that you're doing something right but it's much more helpful to have more detailed comments about *what* it is specifically that you're doing right.

Tell your fellow students over coffee that you think it was a better lecture than usual. This is a pretty common response but it doesn't do anything to help you sustain and develop the improvement in your teaching.

Do nothing. Sadly, this is probably the most common response. What does it do to improve the value of the teaching that you get? You've got it, nothing.

• •

Responses To SAQs, Chapter 10

Response 10.1

You probably surprised yourself. Depending on the subject you may well have jotted down 10 or 20 short questions.

Now, before returning to the text (and without looking at your source material), spend a couple of minutes as follows: look at each question in turn, and put an asterisk beside those that you can't yet answer.

• •

Response 10.2

Here are some of the extra sources you can use to extend your question bank to make it all the more comprehensive and useful. (This is a long response; please study it carefully, we're trying to share several important ideas here.)

Exam questions from past papers

Actually, if your mini-questions are sufficiently all-embracing, they will build up to cover all possible exam questions. However, it's still useful to have real exam questions available. Real questions give you something extra: they help you see how much you're expected to be able to do in a given time. For example, you can tell from them how much you may be asked to do in, say, half an hour during an exam.

It should be possible for you to break down any exam question into the mini-questions you need to be able to handle. One exam question could be an aggregate of 10 or 20 mini-questions. For example: *'Give an illustrated discussion of the corrosion of iron.'*

The short questions you may need to be able to handle to do this exam-type question justice could include (depending on the level of the course):

- Define corrosion
- What three things are necessary for corrosion to happen?
- List four conditions which accelerate corrosion
- Sketch the Pourbaix diagram for iron

10.2 *continued*
- What are the products of iron corrosion?
- Sketch the mechanism of corrosion of a bridge support
- Name six methods of corrosion protection.

Breaking down old exam questions into their component parts usually gives quite a few useful additions to your collection of mini-questions. This means you have more chance of practising your answers to such questions and more guarantee of success in coming exams.

Learning objectives or competence statements
Sometimes, you'll be given lists of syllabus objectives, or your syllabus may list statements of the competences you're to acquire. These say 'at the end of the course, you should be able to ...' with all sorts of completions of that sentence. They are a direct answer to that question 'What am I (reasonably) expected to become able to do?'

Some lecturers will give you objectives for each lecture. 'By the end of this lecture, you should be able to...' and so on.

Objectives can be directly slotted into your question bank. You may prefer, of course, to break down any rather complex objective into its component parts. What you want is to know all the details of what you're expected to master. If you can do all the little things, you're automatically able to do several of them together, and master more complex things.

Worked examples in class
Your lecturers will often solve problems, or run through case-studies, as examples of the sort of thing you're going to be asked to do yourself. What happens, though, if you look back at such a worked example in your lecture notes? Your eyes have hardly started to read the question when they skip ahead to see how it was answered. This robs you of the chance of really finding out whether you can do the problem by yourself.

The remedy is simple: separate the question from its answer. Put the question itself into your question bank, maybe with a reference telling you where you can find the answer in your lecture notes. You are then able to have a go at the question, and then look back to see how well you did.

Homework

'Homework' sounds a bit like school! However, it doesn't stop when you get into college education. It may be called different things, like 'assignments', 'coursework', 'projects', 'essays' and such like, but it's still homework. Most homework starts with some sort of question (even if the question is simply a title). You can easily separate the question from your answer, and file the question separately in your question bank. As with worked examples in class, having the question separate gives you the chance to have another go at the question for practice, without seeing the answer prematurely.

Clues

Often, in a lecture, you'll get the feeling 'the lecturer seems to be plugging this'. It could well be that there is a question coming up on the thing being plugged. You'll get better at spotting such clues, as you get to know your lecturers. It's all too easy to forget which things seemed like clues. But there's a safe way to store them: turn them into questions, and store the questions. This allows you to rehearse your answers to all the things you had the feeling were hinted at by your lecturers.

Other people's question banks

This is something you can do if you've got a few friends studying the same subjects as yourself. Suppose you and a few friends each make a question bank on a given topic. Suppose next, you pool your ideas on what may be the things that you're expected to become able to do. You'll probably find that each member of the group thinks of some questions that no one else thinks of! If you then pool your question banks, and add on those extra questions, the resultant question bank will be quite a bit more comprehensive.

• •

Response 10.3

The clues or prompts which people make are often weird and wonderful! What matters is that they work for you. The more memorable the clues are, the less trouble you'll have bridging the gaps between clues and answers.

Memory can work well by association. Question–answer is one level of association – two-way. But if neither questions nor answers are particularly memorable it can fail. Question–clues–answer is three-way association, and if the clues are particularly memorable (funny?) the whole thing works better.

You've now been through the motions of starting off a question bank. But don't just leave it at that. The logical thing to do is to build the technique into your everyday way of working.

You'll soon find out that making question banks – and practising with them – are both tasks with a high learning payoff.

• •

Response 10.4

Bin it! Tempting, but this won't do you any good. In fact, you'll be losing valuable opportunities.

Feel bad about the score, and too angry to read the feedback comments. Understandable perhaps, but, again, it's not a constructive approach to take.

Feel bad about the score, and quite argumentative about the feedback comments. This is a real danger. A low score or grade can colour your reactions so that you become blind to the value of comments your tutor has written on your work.

Forget the score, and look carefully for what you could glean from the feedback comments. This is the wise approach. Probably the score or grade doesn't count for much in reality, but the things you could learn from finding out exactly why the result was poor could help you prepare effectively for the next time you put together some written work. Also, feedback comments from tutors help you find out about exactly what examiners will be looking for. It's hard to take this positive approach, but we recommend you cultivate it.

• •

Response 10.5

Would you have the courage to tell your friend? It probably all depends on how you would expect your friend to react. It probably all depends how well you knew the person concerned, and so on. How equivocal was your response to our question?

Now let's reverse the situation. Suppose *you* had bad breath; what would you rather happen to you?

- Be told directly
- Receive an anonymous note
- Not be told.

How equivocal was your response in this case? Which do you think is most likely, and what does this tell you about your attitude to receiving feedback?

• •

Responses To SAQs, Chapter 11

Response 11.1

Here are our views on how relevant or otherwise each of those ten things are to exam results.

1 **How much I know.** Exams results are a limited measure of this. Think of all the things you know that aren't asked!

2 **The quantity of revision I've done.** Exam results do reflect this, but less strongly than several of the other things below.

3 **How intelligent I am.** If that's all exams measured, there wouldn't be much point preparing for them. Exams measure various *skills* more than just intelligence.

4 **The quality of revision I've done.** Yes, exam results are very much connected to the quality of revision. Later in this chapter we'll go into what makes 'high-quality' revision.

5 **How much practice I've had at answering exam questions.** Yes indeed, your exam results reflect this. But don't get the practice by taking exams over and over again – there are better ways. More about these later in the chapter.

6 **How well I can spot exam questions.** Spotting questions can be a useful bonus, but it's not safe enough to base your revision policy on this. Playing the spotting game can increase your anxiety about the exam. You'll find yourself wondering 'What will I do if those expected questions don't turn up on the exam paper?'

7 **How quickly I can write in exams.** Many people worry about this. *Quality* of answer is usually far more important than quantity.

8 **How good I am at managing my time in exams.** This is indeed important. Many exam failures are caused by people mismanaging their time during those vital hours – for example only answering three questions when five are required, and so on.

9 **How good I am at addressing the question in exams.** This is probably the most important one. If you go off at tangents, you gain few (if any) extra marks, and waste your time and energy. Sticking to the question is a key skill.

10 **How much I managed to learn the night before!** Some people's exam results are a measure of this. However, tackling exams this way has to be the most dangerous and painful of all the ways you could choose.

• •

Response 11.2

I manage to put if off for ages, until it's really rather too late. You're like many people – too many! Every time you do this you probably say to yourself 'I'll start earlier next time!' Leaving revision till too late is the most painful, and the most risky strategy.

I start gently quite early, then build up to high efforts as the exam gets nearer. This is what most people seem to do. But there are still dangers – for example, you may be tiring yourself out so that during the exam you are too exhausted to perform at your best.

I forget things easily, so I deliberately leave revision till near the exam. We challenge you that this is an excuse rather than a good reason! True, we all forget a lot of what we learn. However, the second time you learn something, it sticks better, and takes less time to learn than the first time. And so on. The more times you've forgotten something, the less likely you are to forget it again. So it's worth starting early and giving yourself the chance to find out what you're likely to forget. This is far better than finding out what you've forgotten when you can't handle an exam question!

I don't do any special 'revision', I work steadily all the time and don't need an extra boost near the exam. If you chose this option, you should be feeling rather pleased with yourself. However, the *kind* of steady work you do needs to change as the exam gets near. Read on to see if you've cracked that one too.

Response 11.3

1   **Reading and rereading all your notes and books.** This is hard work! It's time-consuming, and not very efficient. It's also lonely – you can't really do it with friends. How much of what we read do we remember? Not a lot. *Low* quality.

2   **Digging in the library to find as many extra sources of information as you can.** This can be counter-productive. You're going to be tested on the *main* content of your syllabus. All the extra things you discover may be interesting, but won't be worth much in terms of exam marks. Sad, isn't it? Low quality on the whole. May be better with friends – economy of effort!

3   **Writing out your notes again and again.** This does work. But it's ineffective after a while – and lonely and time-consuming. Only medium quality at best.

4   **Looking through old exam papers and trying to spot likely questions.** This is quite useful in its way, but should only be a small part of your revision policy. On its own, low quality. May be higher quality if done with friends, where you can discuss things.

5   **Practising answering questions, sometimes mentally, sometimes in note form, sometimes in full, sometimes against the clock.** High quality. After all, exams measure your ability to answer exam questions. The more practice you've had at it, the better you become at doing it. Even better if done with other people. Another reason for practising answering questions is that it is easier to develop new behaviours in the safe environment of practising exam questions than in the stressful conditions of the real exam.

6   **Working through your materials, devising your own questions, and practising answering them.** High quality; very high often, especially if done in a small group of fellow students. If you're looking out for possible questions all the time, you're putting yourself in the position of becoming able to answer most questions – not just the ones that have already been set as exam questions.

7 **Working with fellow students, quizzing each other on likely questions.**
This can be high-quality revision – you can cover more ground in an hour of
this sort of activity than you would have done working alone. Also, fellow
students will know when you're trying to waffle!

8 **Getting someone who doesn't know anything about your subject to quiz
you on it (giving them a list of questions to ask you of course!).** This can,
surprisingly enough, also be high quality. Even when the person who
quizzes you doesn't know the right answers, he or she can usually tell
whether you're trying to spin a yarn. The main thing is that *you* will know
which bits need some extra attention.

9 **Building a glossary for your subject material.** This can be high quality,
especially if done with friends. It's a way of covering a lot of ground in a
short time and having something useful to show for your efforts.

10 **Prioritising key points for each section of a topic.** This can be high quality,
because it keeps you in decision-making mode – in other words, active.
Better still if done with friends: two minds are better than one at this, and so
on.

11 **Making a list of concepts, and for each concept identifying as many uses
as you can.** This is high quality, especially when done with friends. It's a
good way of getting to understand things.

●●

Response 11.4

Here are six things that you could do in the first ten minutes of an exam, before
starting your first answer.

Before even reading any of the questions:

- Write your name, and/or other details (such as subject, candidate
  number, date, place – whatever's asked for) in the appropriate places on
  the exam book. (Maybe half-a-minute.) There are always some
  anonymous scripts handed in – often good ones!
- Check that you've got the right question paper! (Two seconds)

- Find out how many questions you've got to do, and whether, for example, you've got to choose two from Section A, one from Section B and so on. (Five seconds)
- Check whether or not the questions carry equal marks. (Five seconds)
- Subtract half an hour from the total time available (these first ten minutes, and 20 minutes to be saved for the end), then work out a rough timetable showing at what time you should be moving on to your second, third, etc question. (Spend a minute or two on this, get it right)
- Now start reading the questions.

•••

Response 11.5

It isn't just 'reading' is it?   It's decision-making time as well.

- Read each question *slowly,* and more than once
- Work out exactly what the question is asking for
- Underline or highlight key 'process' words (such as discuss, describe, evaluate, compare, contrast, calculate, define, prove, analyse...)
- Circle key 'content' words. You can then quickly tell the difference at a glance between the key 'content' words and the 'process' words
- (Optional.) Maybe scribble down a few words to remind you of relevant key ideas that you don't want to forget, should you choose the question
- Look back at each question with this in mind: 'Is this a good question for *me?'* If it's very good for you put two ticks beside it. If it's fairly good, put one tick. If it's no good, put a cross beside it. Then you can make a sensible choice about which questions you'll do, and in which order to try them. (Most people like to start with a good one!)

•••

Response 11.6

What are the 'wrong' things to do just after an exam? Well, what normally happens outside an exam room after it's over? What's it called?   The *post-mortem.* It couldn't have a better name in fact. The exam is now dead!   There's nothing at all you can do about it any more. So why waste your mental energy going over it all once again? Think of the chatter:

'Did you do question 5?'

'What did you get for the answer?'

'I didn't get that.'

'Did you remember to ...?'

The more you listen, the more you feel that everyone else has done wonderfully and you've done terribly! By now, the people who actually did do well are probably doing something much more sensible.

In fact, if you indulge in a post-mortem, you're a masochist! You're choosing to relive the whole exam, perhaps in painful slow motion. A post-mortem may help you learn moree about the topic, but it can't improve that exam score.

What's the sensible alternative? Well, get away from that group for a start. You need a rest, but probably need to wind down a bit before you can really relax. Have a go at this. Use some summary notes or question-bank lists connected with your next exam for half an hour, gently doing a bit of revision for that. You may get the pleasantest of feelings: that of gently replacing all the information that was in your mind for the past exam with things you'll need for that next exam. After a little of this gentle revision, you'll be ready to have that rest. *And* you'll be much happier than if you'd done a post-mortem.

References And Further Reading

Fairbairn, G J and Winch, C (1993) *Reading, Writing and Reasoning: A guide for students*, SRHE/Open University Press, Buckingham.

Hector-Taylor, M and Bonsall, M (1993) *Successful Study: A practical way to get a degree*, Hallamshire Press, Sheffield.

Jeffers, S (1987) *Feel the Fear and Do It Anyway*, Century Hutchinson, London.

Larson, T (1979) *Trust Yourself*, Impact Publishers, San Luis Obispo, CA.

Mirsky, N (1994) *The Unforgettable Memory Book*, BBC/Penguin, Harmondsworth.

Northedge, A (1990) *The Good Study Guide*, Open University Press, Buckingham.

Race, P (1992) *500 Tips for Students*, Blackwell, Oxford.

Race, P (1995) *Who Learns Wins*, BBC/Penguin, Harmondsworth.

Rowntree, D (1988) *Learn How to Study – A guide for students of all ages*, Kogan Page, London.

Walter, T and Siebert, A (1987) *Student Success: How to succeed at college and still have time for your friends*, Holt, Rinehart and Winston, New York.

Index

We've made a short index to help you track down some of the key ideas in our book. We haven't included in the index any of the ideas contained in our *Responses* to all the SAQs, however. We think the best way for you to find these ideas is after having a go at the questions, rather than from an index.

action plan for studying   42–3
action plan for revision   123–5
active learning   12, 81–90
aims of studying   19
asking questions in class   94–5
assessment   95–6
attitudes towards tutors   98–100

brainstorming   76

challenges   140–42
college resources   28
competence   45–53
concentrating   60
conceptual skills   34–5
criticism, *see* feedback,   111

danger box   50–51
difficulties of studying   22
digesting, making sense of learning
   14
drop-out   138–9

efficient studying   70–80
egg diagrams   75–8
encouragement   31

essay planning   76–8
exams   82–3, 116–17, 128–37

family commitments   23
feedback   13, 14, 110–15
feedback from tutors   110–11
feedback to Tom and Phil   148–9
feelings   13
feelings about tutors   92–3
feelings before exams   126
fellow students   30
friends   23, 87–8

Gardner, Howard   39
getting started   70–71

Handy, Charles   39
home resources   31

improving your tutors   100–102
intelligence   39–40

job commitments   23, 143–4
jug and mug approach   89–90

Larson, Tony   140

'lay an egg' technique 75–8
learning toolkit 87
lecturers 92

magic box 51–2
mental blanks 134
mid-course blues 142–3
morale 143

odd places and study 66
opportunities 54
other people 25, 41, 56

panic in exams 134
passive learning 82
personal development aims 20
personal skills 33–9
pitfalls 22
places to study 64–9
positive feelings 13
practice 14
purposes for learning 17

question banks 107–10
questions to tutors 93–5

reading limbo 79
reasons for learning 17
resources 27
revision 117–26

self-analysis questions: purposes 12,
 14
schedule, keeping to 61
social skills 37–9
space audit 68
spurts 62
strengths 54
support network 41–2
SWOT analysis 53–6

target box 48
teachers 91
technical skills 36
threats 54
time audit 58–9
time management 23, 57–63
time management in exams 130–34
transit box 49
trial and error 12
tutors 91–104

uncompetence 46
unsuccessful learning 13

wanting to learn 14, 15
weaknesses 54
work versus **WORK** 72–5
workplace resources 32
worrying 127